ITALIAN FOOD, FAMILY AND FOOLISHNESS II

ITALIAN FOOD, FAMILY AND FOOLISHNESS II

by
The Old Uncle and The Nephew
Paul Provenzano & Nash D'Amico, Jr.

Published by Paul Joe Provenzano Publishing

First Edition January 2002

ISBN 0-9672259-3-0
$14.95

Printed in the United States of America

From the Nephew

For two very special roses in my life, my mother, Rosalie and my daughter, Brina Rose.

To my mother, who played such an important role in the development of my taste buds. It was your continued exposure to great Italian cooking and family dishes that inspired a desire to make food a career.

To my beautiful daughter, Brina, the apple of my eye and the true food of my life. I have been truly blessed with the privilege of raising such a wonderful and genuine person. This year we reached a milestone when I gave your hand in marriage - but just the hand, I'll hold on to the rest.

God Bless, and Buon Appetito,
Nash, D'Amico, Jr.
"The Nephew"

From the Old Uncle

I would like to dedicate my part of this book to the two finest women I have ever known.

First, to my lovely wife, Esther Mae, who has dedicated 59 wonderful years to me and our son.

Second, to my beautiful mother, Jennie Provenzano, who devoted her life to my father and their three sons.

All my love to them.
Paul Joe Provenzano
"The Old Uncle"

Ah, Italy!

The Old Uncle at the bakery on Dumble Street.

The Nephew & The Old Uncle, taste-testing the latest recipes.

ITALY - The home of the Roman Empire! The land of the conquerors. What a change time can make. Today it's the land of romance and food.

Food? Yes, food. FOOD.

That's the magic word for the Nephew and the Old Uncle. Oh, they are both romantics, have no doubt about that, but food has been the primary part of both of their lives. The Nephew has been into the restaurant business since graduation from college. Yes, he's been in the food business ever since and that's probably a lot more years than that deceptively good-looking face shows.

The Old Uncle? Well, he doesn't discuss age anymore. He recently had his hair cut down to a burr because he can't see to comb it. At age seven, he was frying doughnuts for his dad. At fourteen, he was a full fledged baker. The eye doctor vetoed his attempt at college so he remained in the bakery business for twenty years past his graduation from high school.

In the Food Section, The Nephew and the Old Uncle overcame the teasing and pooled their knowledge, in addition to spending a great length of time doing the necessary research to assure themselves of giving the readers an outstanding book. Those recipes considered untouchables were repeated but for the most part, everything else is new.

The Family Section has been added because they believe it will add much color to the book, besides some very old, old recipes.

Now we get to the Foolishness Section. Cajun recipes in an Italian cookbook? That's foolishness, right? But they're in there. There's more foolishness too, you'll see.

The Three Ingrando sisters– Jennie D'Amico, Rosie Bilao and Annie Ligotino.

The D'Amico's Sunday gathering around the dining table.

The Old Uncle and his son, Joe Provenzano, outside the family bakery.

TABLE OF CONTENTS

For Individual Recipes - See Recipe Index in back of the book

SECTION ONE
FOOD

PART ONE: SAUCES

The Body and Soul of Italian Cooking

***THE NEPHEW AND THE OLD UNCLE** were relaxed in the open patio front of the D'AMICO'S ITALIAN MARKET CAFE.*

"Quite a layout, you got here, Nephew. You and your partner, Luke, have it all here. Free Parking, very sensible prices, delicious food, well, I could go on but you'd get a swelled head. In fact, you already have one."

"You know, Old Uncle, you were doing fairly well for a while there, in fact, it's made me happy considering it came from you."

The Old Uncle laughed and continued: "Why don't you open up some of that good wine you been braggin' about. I'm dry as a desert flower."

"One thing's certain, you're no flower period." Then the Nephew snapped his finger, and a bus boy came running over. "Bring us a bottle of that new Chianti."

Soon the pair were sipping on a glass of the wine. "Nephew, you got some new sauces for our new book?"

"Oh, sure. Some classics. How about you?"

"Three new ones. One's a beautiful smooth white."

"From you, Old Uncle, I never expected you saying anything else. Damn good sauce, lotsa braggin' with it."

"I'm gonna ignore part of that. I have a great red sauce with pork. Even you will have to have seconds."

"Old Man, you are a card. Anyway, besides a few changes on my standards, I have a couple of new light red sauces."

"Nephew, just be sure the Alfredo sauce is in there."

"Oh, it's in there. I know you love that particular white one."

Grandma Ester D'Amico and three sons - Tony, Frank & Nick.

The Pizzitola family, gathered around Paw Paw Charlie (seated).

The Nephew's daughter, Brina (center), smiles big for her wedding day!

THE NEPHEW'S ITALIAN SUGA SAUCE II

Servings — Unless you have a large family or a house party, this recipe is sufficient for you to freeze some of it. Sauces freeze very well, so you can enjoy it several times without all the initial cooking.

To freeze, we suggest placing 12 oz. sauce in each carton, which would be enough for two people. At this figure, the recipe makes 25 servings. Also, if you go all out and make meatballs, you could add four meatballs to each carton. The Nephew's Meatball Recipe will make about 40 of those delicious little gems

INGREDIENTS & UTENSILS

- ❐ 1 large ONION
- ❐ 12 cloves Fresh GARLIC
- ❐ 1/2 cup OLIVE OIL
- ❐ 1 Tbls Fresh BASIL or 1 teas Dried
- ❐ 1 Tbls SALT
- ❐ 1 teas Dried OREGANO
- ❐ 1/4 teas WHITE PEPPER
- ❐ 4-12 oz cans CRUSHED TOMATOES
- ❐ 8- 12 oz cans TOMATO SAUCE
- ❐ 14- oz dry RED WINE
- ❐ Add Salt and Pepper for final seasoning
- ❐ Chopping block and knife
- ❐ 6 qt pot for cooking sauce
- ❐ Large spoon
- ❐ Freezer cartons *(if you need them)*

Happy birthday, Bubby! The Nephew celebrates his 6th birthday!

THE NEPHEW'S ITALIAN SUGA SAUCE II

Notes - Suga or Red Sauce. Call it what you like but it's the king of Italian Sauces in popularity

Method of Preparation

Rinse and chop:

- 1 Large ONION
- 12 cloves Fresh GARLIC

In a 6 qt pot, add 1/2 cup OLIVE OIL.

Heat and then add the above onion and garlic.

Saute until onions are translucent

Reduce heat and add:

- 1 Tbls Fresh BASIL or 1 teas dried
- 1 Tbls SALT
- 1 teas DRIED OREGANO
- 1/4 teas WHITE PEPPER

Cook 2 minutes, add:

- 4 - 12 oz cans CRUSHED TOMATOES
- 8 - 12 oz cans TOMATO SAUCE

Simmer 1 hour stirring occasionally

Add 14 oz dry RED WINE

If you are making meatballs the same day, now would be the time to add them. Also, if you want to add ground beef or pork instead, be sure to brown it first.

Now, simmer for 3 hours, stirring occasionally

It's time to taste your prize venture. If you think it needs salt, or pepper, or both, add it. You're the chef now!

Delicious. Time consuming but worth it.

THE NEPHEW'S POMODORI SAUCE

Servings - 4

A Delightful Light Tomato Sauce

INGREDIENTS & UTENSILS

- ❒ 12-14 ROMA TOMATOES
- ❒ 4 oz Extra Virgin OLIVE OIL
- ❒ 4 oz minced GARLIC
- ❒ 1 teas BLACK PEPPER
- ❒ 1 teas WHITE PEPPER
- ❒ 1 teas SEASONING SALT
- ❒ 2 oz Fresh Chopped BASIL
- ❒ Roasting pan
- ❒ Tomato mill or blender and strainer
- ❒ Large skillet and Spoon

METHOD OF PREPARATION

Roast the 12 - 14 ROMA TOMATOES in a large roasting pan, standing in about 1 inch of tap water.

Bake in a 350 degree oven for about 25 minutes, until tomatoes are soft and well roasted. Pour water off.

Put tomatoes through a tomato mill or in a blender, and follow this by putting them through a strainer.

In a hot skillet, add 4 oz OLIVE OIL and 4 oz minced GARLIC. Cook for 2 minutes.

Add Tomato mixture, 1 teas each of WHITE PEPPER, BLACK PEPPER, and SEASONING SALT and 2 oz Fresh Chopped BASIL.

Cook until reduced by 20 percent.

THE NEPHEW'S ALFREDO SAUCE

Servings - 2

The amazing heavy cream sauce no one ever forgets. If you are making Fettuccini Alfredo, turn to the pasta entree recipe and follow this recipe for the sauce.

INGREDIENTS & UTENSILS

- ❒ 12 oz HEAVY CREAM
- ❒ 4 Tbls BUTTER or MARGARINE
- ❒ 8 oz Grated ROMANO CHEESE
- ❒ Saute pan and spoon

METHOD OF PREPARATION

In a saute pan, place :

- 12 oz HEAVY CREAM
- 4 Tbls BUTTER or MARGARINE
- 8 oz Grated ROMANO CHEESE

Stir on low to medium heat until reduced by 1/3.

That's all there is to it. Very easy for such a magnificent sauce. If not ready to use now, it may be refrigerated.

6-year old Bubby (Nash, the Nephew) waves to the camera.

THE OLD UNCLE'S VELVET WHITE SAUCE

Servings - 3 - 4
Cook Fettuccini or Linguini pasta, and add this sauce if desired. Similar to Fettuccini Alfredo, but with less fat. An easy one.

INGREDIENTS & UTENSILS

- ❒ 3 Tbls Melted BUTTER
- ❒ 1 cup Canned SKIM MILK
- ❒ 2 Tbls Grated ROMANO CHEESE
- ❒ 1 heaping teas ARROWROOT*
- ❒ 1 teas Dried BASIL or 3 Fresh
- ❒ Pinches of SALT and WHITE PEPPER
- ❒ 1 cup WHIPPING CREAM
- ❒ 3 Tbls Grated ROMANO CHEESE
- ❒ 2 teas Dried Basil or 6 Fresh
- ❒ Large to medium skillet and large spoon

METHOD OF PREPARATION

In a skillet, melt 3 Tbls BUTTER, cooking until light brown.

Remove from fire, add following ingredients:

- 1 cup Canned SKIM MILK
- 2 Tbls Grated ROMANO CHEESE
- 1 heaping teas ARROWROOT*
- 1 teas Dried BASIL or 3 Fresh
- Pinch of SALT and WHITE PEPPER

Cook until it thickens some, and few bubbles appear.

Remove from fire and add:

- 1 cup WHIPPING CREAM
- 3 Tbls Grated ROMANO CHEESE
- 2 teas Dried BASIL or 6 Fresh

Cook again, stirring often, until it thickens and a few bubbles appear. You can save sauce until later if you didn't boil the pasta. Refrigerate it, if not used right away. Then warm it.

**Arrowroot - a thickening agent sold in the spice section*

THE NEPHEW'S MARINARA SAUCE

INGREDIENTS & UTENSILS

- ❒ 4- 12 oz cans Whole PEELED TOMATOES
- ❒ 6 - cloves Fresh GARLIC
- ❒ 1/4 cup Fresh PARSLEY discarding stems
- ❒ 1/4 cup Fresh BASIL
- ❒ 1/8 cup OLIVE OIL
- ❒ 3/4 teas SALT
- ❒ 1/4 teas WHITE PEPPER
- ❒ Blender or Food Processor
- ❒ Chopping board and knife
- ❒ Large pot and spoon
- ❒ Cartons for freezing if desired

Servings - 11

A sauce somewhat lighter than the heartier Red Suga Sauce. This recipe is from our first Italian Food Family and Foolishness. The only difference is that it has been reduced in half. Now, it's 64 oz, enough to put up 5 cartons of 12 oz with each carton serving 2 people.

Baby Nash (The Nephew) and his older brother, Frank.

The Old Uncle's son, JP and his wife, Linda.

Continued on next page following!

THE NEPHEW'S MARINARA SAUCE

Continued

METHOD OF PREPARATION

Liquefy in a blender :

- 4 - 12 oz cans Whole PEELED TOMATOES

Set aside.

Chop finely the easiest way :

- 6 cloves Fresh GARLIC
- 1/4 cup Fresh PARSLEY, discarding stems

Coarsely chop *(1/4 inch or smaller)*:

- 1/4 cup Fresh BASIL

Divide Basil in half, placing half with the Garlic and Parsley, reserving the balance.

In a large pot on medium high heat, add:

- 1/8 cup OLIVE OIL

Add the Garlic, Parsley, and Basil mixture and saute.

Add the Tomatoes, reduce heat to medium, and cook for one hour stirring frequently. Now add the remaining half of the Basil.

Gradually add while tasting :

- 3/4 teas SALT
- 1/4 teas WHITE PEPPER

Simmer for 1 1/2 hours, checking seasoning while stirring occasionally. Use on selected recipe, freezing the balance.

THE NEPHEW'S TAGLIERINI SAUCE

Servings - 4

Similar to Pomodori Sauce. This one has less Garlic but has Fresh Basil added. It depends on what you prefer. Both are very good.

INGREDIENTS & UTENSILS

- ❒ 12 ROMA TOMATOES
- ❒ 2 ounces OLIVE OIL
- ❒ 2 ounces Fresh Sliced GARLIC
- ❒ 1 teas BLACK PEPPER
- ❒ 1 teas WHITE PEPPER
- ❒ 1 teas SEASONED SALT
- ❒ 2 ounces Fresh Chopped BASIL
- ❒ Roasting Pan
- ❒ Sharp Knife
- ❒ Food Processor or Blender

METHOD OF PREPARATION

In a Roasting Pan, place the 12 ROMA TOMATOES in about an inch of tap water.

Cover with:

- 2 ounces OLIVE OIL
- 2 ounces Fresh Sliced GARLIC
- 1 teas each of BLACK PEPPER, WHITE PEPPER & SEASONED SALT.
- 2 ounces Fresh Chopped BASIL

Bake for about 25 minutes in oven at 350 degrees until tomatoes are soft and well roasted.

Let cool.

Now, place it all in a Food Processor, and process only until it is coarsely chopped.

Delicious over cooked hot pasta or any recipe of your choice.

THE OLD UNCLE'S MEAT SAUCE ITALIA

Servings - 12 - 14
Unless you are planning a party, get your freezer cartons out, as we plan to take care of your needs for a real first class Italian sauce.

Ingredients & Utensils

- ❒ 2 lbs Fresh ROMA TOMATOES chopped or 2 - 14 1/2 oz cans Fresh chopped TOMATOES
- ❒ 12 cloves Fresh GARLIC, sliced thin
- ❒ 2 Tbls OLIVE OIL
- ❒ 2 teas DRIED BASIL
- ❒ 2 -8 oz cans TOMATO PASTE
- ❒ 32 oz tap WATER
- ❒ 4 - 8 oz cans TOMATO SAUCE
- ❒ 2 Medium ONIONS, chopped fine
- ❒ 5 Tbls Grated ROMANO CHEESE
- ❒ 5 Tbls SUGAR
- ❒ 1 Tbls DRIED BASIL
- ❒ 1 Tbls DRIED OREGANO
- ❒ 4 teas BEEF BOUILLON POWDER
- ❒ 1 -1/2 lbs GROUND PORK, lean
- ❒ 2 teas GROUND CHIPOTLE CHILES or RED PEPPER
- ❒ 2 teas SALT
- ❒ 2 teas each Dried OREGANO and BASIL
- ❒ Roasting pan
- ❒ Sharp knife
- ❒ Large pot and spoon

Method of Preparation

In a roasting pan, sprayed with vegetable oil, place:

- 2 lbs chopped Fresh ROMA TOMATOES
- 12 cloves Fresh GARLIC, sliced thin
- 2 Tbls OLIVE OIL *(drizzle over above)*
- 2 teas DRIED BASIL *(sprinkle over above)*

Note - If Chipotle Chiles are not available, use Ground Red Pepper

THE OLD UNCLE'S MEAT SAUCE ITALIA

Continued

Place into oven at 350 degrees for 30 minutes.

Set Aside.

In a large pot, place:

- 2 - 8 oz cans TOMATO PASTE
- 32 oz tap WATER
- 4 - 8 oz cans TOMATO SAUCE
- 2 Medium ONIONS, chopped fine
- 5 Tbls Grated ROMANO CHEESE
- 5 Tbls SUGAR
- 1 Tbls DRIED BASIL
- 1 Tbls DRIED OREGANO
- 4 teas BEEF BOUILLON POWDER

The Old Uncles' grandson, Dan and his lovely wife, Traci.

Bring to a boil, reduce heat and simmer for 2 hours.Add Fresh Tomato-Garlic-Olive Oil-Basil Mixture.

Bring back to a boil, lower heat and simmer for 1 hour.

Add: 1 1/2 lbs Ground PORK.

Bring back to a boil, lower heat and simmer for 1 hour.

Add:

- 2 teas of Dried OREGANO and BASIL
- 2 teas Ground CHIPOLTE CHILES or Red Pepper
- 2 teas SALT

The Old Uncle's grandson, Gary, with his wife, Pam.

Cook for 1/2 hour on low heat or simmer.

Enjoy! This recipe takes time but it will be very rewarding

THE NEPHEW'S BECHAMEL SAUCE

Servings - 6 - Highly recommended for the Cannolloni Entree, although it can be used on many other ones.

INGREDIENTS & UTENSILS

- ❒ 4 Tbls BUTTER or MARGARINE
- ❒ 4 Tbls FLOUR
- ❒ 1 qt MILK *(whole, low fat or skim)*
- ❒ 1/2 Onion *(cut into 3 pieces)*
- ❒ 2 - 3 Bay Leaves
- ❒ 1 teas SALT
- ❒ 1/4 teas NUTMEG
- ❒ 9 inch sauce pan
- ❒ 1/2 gal pan or pot
- ❒ Knife and cutting board
- ❒ Wire whisk and strainer

METHOD OF PREPARATION

In a sauce pan, melt 4 oz BUTTER or MARGARINE. Being careful the butter does not brown or burn.

Add: 4 oz FLOUR gradually.

Mix continuously over low heat until it becomes the color of walnuts. *(About 2-4 minutes)* Set aside.

Moisten the bottom of a 1/2 gallon pan or pot with about an ounce of water. This will help keep the milk from burning.

Add:

- 1 qt MILK *(whole, low-fat, or skim)*
- 1/2 Medium ONION cut in 3 pieces
- 2 or 3 BAY LEAVES
- 1 teas SALT
- 1/4 teas NUTMEG

Note- A mild rich sauce with a marvelous flavor

THE NEPHEW'S BECHAMEL SAUCE

Continued

Cook on medium to low heat until it gets warm but DO NOT LET IT BOIL.

At this point, whisk in the previously made roux, a little at a time. Cook for 4 minutes, stirring continually. Remove from fire. Strain.

If any part of this sauce is burned, it will give it an off or bitter taste, spoiling it.

Now, you are ready for the Cannelloni or what ever you want to do with it.

The Nephew's Great-grandmother Ester D'Amico (Her maiden name was Fasulla and she immigrated from Corleone, Sicily.)

Maw Maw Jennie & Paw Paw Frank with the infant Nephew (Nash, Jr.)

THE NEPHEW'S MOSTARDA SAUCE

A rich mustard cream sauce.

Servings - 4 - An easy to prepare class dish. Can be made at the same time you prepare the Chicken Mostarda recipe, or ahead of time if you so prefer.

INGREDIENTS & UTENSILS

❒ 1 oz OLIVE OIL
❒ 4 ROMA TOMATOES, Diced
❒ 3 Tbls BUTTER or MARGARINE
❒ 3 teas POMMERY MUSTARD
❒ 12 oz HEAVY WHIPPING CREAM
❒ 1 oz Fresh BASIL, Chopped
❒ 1 teas each BLACK & WHITE PEPPER
❒ 1 teas SEASONING SALT
❒ Large skillet and spoon

METHOD OF PREPARATION

In a large skillet, heat 1 oz OLIVE OIL

Add: 4 ROMA TOMATOES Diced

Saute for about 2 minutes.

Add: 3 Tbls BUTTER, stir

Then add 3 teas POMMERY MUSTARD, stir.

Then add:

- 12 oz WHIPPING CREAM
- 1 teas each BLACK & WHITE PEPPER
- 1 teas SEASONING SALT

Incorporate or blend together, and cook until reduced slightly.

Now you are ready to make the CHICKEN MOSTARDA recipe or any other one you have in mind.

THE OLD UNCLE'S ITALIAN RED SAUCE II

INGREDIENTS & UTENSILS

- ❒ 3 12 oz cans TOMATO PASTE
- ❒ 6 cups tap WATER
- ❒ 5 8 oz cans TOMATO SAUCE
- ❒ 8 oz dry RED WINE
- ❒ 2 Medium ONIONS finely chopped
- ❒ 5 Tbls Grated ROMANO CHEESE
- ❒ 5 Tbls SUGAR
- ❒ 2 Tbls Dried GARLIC POWDER
- ❒ 1 Tbls Dried BASIL or 3 Fresh
- ❒ 1 Tbls Dried OREGANO or 3 Fresh
- ❒ 6 teas BEEF BOUILLON POWDER
- ❒ 6 oz SUN-DRIED TOMATOES blanched and chopped
- ❒ 1 Tbls Grated ROMANO CHEESE
- ❒ 1 Tbls Dried BASIL or 3 Fresh
- ❒ 2 teas SALT
- ❒ 1 teas BLACK PEPPER
- ❒ Large pot and top *(preferably 8 qt)*
- ❒ Chopping board and knife

METHOD OF PREPARATION

Spray your big pot with Vegetable Spray, and place the following ingredients into it:

- ◆ 3 12 oz cans TOMATO PASTE
- ◆ 6 cups tap WATER
- ◆ 5 8 oz cans TOMATO SAUCE
- ◆ 8 oz dry RED WINE

Use recipe water to clean out tomato paste cans.

Cook on low heat, stirring frequently to avoid sticking, for one hour without the top.

Servings - Figuring about 6 oz of sauce per serving, this recipe should make about 15 servings. Use what you need this time, and freeze the balance as it seems to taste as good or better later. My suggestion is to put 12 oz in each carton, and four meatballs if you also decided to make them. Good Luck.

Note - Follow the cooking instructions close, for you are about to make the best tasting sauce that ever entered my mouth, and I have tasted many

-The Old Uncle.

Continued on the next page following!

THE OLD UNCLE'S ITALIAN RED SAUCE II

Continued

Now add:

- 2 Medium ONIONS, finely chopped
- 5 Tbls Grated ROMANO CHEESE
- 5 Tbls SUGAR
- 2 Tbls GARLIC POWDER
- 1 Tbls DRIED BASIL or 3 Tbls Fresh
- 1 Tbls DRIED OREGANO or 3 Tbls Fresh
- 6 teas BEEF BOUILLON POWDER

Mix well, and simmer for 2 hours, covered for the first hour, then remove the top.

Add 6 oz SUN DRIED TOMATOES, blanched and chopped.

Mix well, leave uncovered and cook for one hour.

Now add:

- 1 Tbls Grated ROMANO CHEESE
- 1 Tbls DRIED BASIL or 3 Tbls Fresh
- 2 teas SALT
- 1 teas BLACK PEPPER

Simmer for 30 minutes, without the top. Taste for seasoning. Add, if necessary, salt, pepper, or whatever. You're the chef now. So do your stuff.

PART TWO: PASTA ENTREES

The Grandaddy of Italian Cooking

The Nephew and the Old Uncle sat at a table next to the wall in the back of the restaurant. The Nephew watched the Old Uncle polish off his plate.

"Don't tell me you want some more?"

"It's good enough for two more helpings, but I've run out of room." The Old Uncle smiled as the waiter removed his plate. "Nephew, That's the best dish in the place."

"You think it's good, so we agree finally."

The Old Uncle sat back. "Mezzaluna. People might have trouble with that name, but once they eat it, they won't forget it."

"You have a new pasta dish for our book?"

"I'm glad I did before I ate that lasagne. It might have scared me off."

"Old Uncle, slow up on the compliments. It doesn't fit your style. You need a favor?"

The Old Uncle just grunted and replied. "When you got it, you got it."

"Okay, I accept your compliments, but you of all people should understand why I'm suspicious. Tell me about your new pasta dish, you have one or not?"

"I have one, my boy, and I like it. It's called The Old Uncle's Something Special. How 'bout that for an entree?"

The Nephew laughed. "Good name but what's in it?"

"A real Italian dish. Linguini pasta covered with Italian goodies. Sun Dried Tomatoes, Sauteed Mushrooms, Artichoke Hearts, plus a few surprises that make it something special. "

"You old fox, you figured to bury me with that dish, and then came today, so you are not so sure, right?"

The Old Uncle was laughing so hard he almost choked. "I'm right, and you know it."

"Not exactly, but close." They smiled at each other.

"What else you got, Nephew?"

"Oh, some other strong ones. You know, the Cannelloni, Lasagne, among others."

"Well, I got a new Lasagne, besides my special."

They sat out on the patio, and the Old Uncle denied he could see a good-looking woman stroll by.

The Nephew laughed. "You know, I realize you have very poor sight. You just cook so well, it's hard to believe. "

"A compliment! I had given up hope."

THE NEPHEW'S SPAGHETTI & MEATBALLS II

The Number one Italian Dish in the Country!

Servings - 20 - This meatball recipe is the same as in our first book. It refers you to make The Nephew's Italian Suga Sauce on the same day you make the meatballs. This recipe makes approximately 40 meatballs, and allowing 2 to a serving, that accounts for the 20 servings. These two recipes would balance out almost perfect. See Note for another suggestion.

Note: If would prefer to cut the meatball recipe in half, you could switch to The Old Uncle's Italian Red Sauce II for your sauce. It would balance out well. Good luck, Chef

INGREDIENTS & UTENSILS

- ❒ 5 lbs lean GROUND BEEF
- ❒ 1 1/2 bunches Fresh PARSLEY chopped
- ❒ 1 1/2 bunches GREEN ONIONS chopped
- ❒ 1/2 cup chopped GARLIC
- ❒ 1/2 Tbls Fresh OREGANO or 1/2 tsp Dried
- ❒ 1/2 Tbls Fresh BASIL or 1/2 teas Dried
- ❒ 1/2 Tbls BLACK PEPPER
- ❒ 1 Tbls SALT
- ❒ 2 cups Grated ROMANO CHEESE
- ❒ 1 1/2 cups Fresh plain BREAD CRUMBS
- ❒ 1 cup MILK
- ❒ 6 EGGS
- ❒ 3-4 oz SPAGHETTI or PASTA per person
- ❒ WATER to boil, salt and olive oil added
- ❒ VEGETABLE SPRAY
- ❒ Chopping board and Knife
- ❒ Large Bowl for mixing
- ❒ Large pan
- ❒ Large pot
- ❒ Measuring scale *(or a good imagination)*

METHOD OF PREPARATION

Combine:

- 5 lbs lean GROUND BEEF
- 1 1/2 bunches Fresh PARSLEY chopped
- 1 1/2 bunches GREEN ONIONS chopped
- 1/4 cup GARLIC chopped
- 1/2 Tbls Fresh OREGANO or 1/2 teas Dried
- 1/2 Tbls Fresh BASIL or 1/2 teas Dried
- 1/2 Tbls BLACK PEPPER
- 1 Tbls SALT

THE NEPHEW'S SPAGHETTI & MEATBALLS II

Continued

- 2 cups Grated ROMANO CHEESE
- 1 1/2 cups Fresh plain BREAD CRUMBS

Add:

- 1 cup MILK
- 6 EGGS

Mix together well by hand. Using a small scale or a great imagination, roll each meatball out to about 3 oz or less. Spray a large flat pan or cookie sheet with VEGETABLE SPRAY. Place the meatballs so as to not touch. Bake at 350 degrees only until slightly brown. Finally, add the meatballs to the sauce the last 3 hours of cooking before you can serve them.

If not making sauce that day, freeze them, remembering they still need about 3 hours of cooking time in the sauce.

At mealtime, add 3-4 oz SPAGHETTI or PASTA to a pot of boiling water that has a little salt and olive oil previously added. Cook until barely done. Pour sauce and add meatballs over spaghetti and serve. Great job, Chef

Spaghetti & Meatballs

THE NEPHEW'S LINGUINI DIAVOLO

Servings - 2 - This recipe calls for Marinara Sauce previously made. If you have either The Nephew's Italian Suga Sauce or The Old Uncle's Italian Red Sauce, you could substitute and not sacrifice any quality. This is a spicy dish with lots of seafood. We would expect you to make some substitutes.

Ingredients & Utensils

- ❒ 4 whole little NECK CLAMS, steamed open
- ❒ 8 whole MUSSELS
- ❒ 8 - 12 CRAB FINGERS depending on size
- ❒ 8 oz steamed SQUID
- ❒ 4 SHRIMP *(16 - 20 size)*
- ❒ 2 oz OLIVE OIL
- ❒ 2 oz fresh GARLIC sliced
- ❒ 2 pinches fresh chopped BASIL
- ❒ 2 pinches crushed RED PEPPER
- ❒ 2 pinches BLACK PEPPER
- ❒ 2 pinches SEASON SALT
- ❒ 2 pinches WHITE PEPPER
- ❒ 4 pieces chopped ANCHOVIES
- ❒ 1 oz chopped GREEN ONIONS
- ❒ 12 oz LINGUINI COOKED
- ❒ 2 oz WHITE WINE
- ❒ 12 whole PIMENTO-STUFFED GREEN OLIVES
- ❒ 9 oz MARINARA SAUCE
- ❒ 9 inch Saute Pan
- ❒ Large pot
- ❒ 2 small platters
- ❒ Pasta Fork
- ❒ Ladle

Method of Preparation

Put 2 oz OLIVE OIL into a Saute pan, and heat until hot.

THE NEPHEW'S LINGUINI DIAVOLO

Continued

Then Add:

- 4 Whole Fresh little NECK CLAMS, steamed
- 8 Whole MUSSELS
- 8 oz Fresh cleaned SQUID
- 4 SHRIMP *(16-20 size)*
- 2 oz Fresh GARLIC, sliced
- 2 pinches Fresh chopped BASIL
- 2 pinches crushed RED PEPPER
- 2 pinches BLACK PEPPER
- 2 pinches SEASONING SALT
- 2 pinches WHITE PEPPER
- 1 oz GREEN ONIONS chopped

Cover and cook for about three minutes until shell fish are open.

Add:

- 8 - 12 CRAB FINGERS
- 2 oz WHITE WINE
- 12 Whole PIMENTO-STUFFED GREEN OLIVES
- 4 pieces ANCHOVIES, chopped
- 9 oz MARINARA SAUCE

Cook about Three minutes.

Boil 12 oz LINGUINI PASTA *(These are large servings)* With a little salt and olive oil added. When done, drain well. Divide the pasta between two warmed platters. Now, arrange the seafood on top of the Linguini, dividing it accordingly. Then pour MARINARA SAUCE over the seafood and the pasta.

A time consuming dish. Yes. Delicious, yes. Remember, you're the chef!

THE OLD UNCLE'S ITALIAN SAUSAGE LASAGNE

Servings - 10

Notes - Adding the Italian Red Sauce to the top of the Lasagne before serving will certainly help this or any other Lasagne. If you don't have red sauce in the freezer, buy a jar from the store, remembering to get it plain with no added vegetables or meat. Lasagne freezes well but be sure to slice the portions.

Ingredients & Utensils

- ❒ 2 lbs GROUND ITALIAN SAUSAGE *(Italian sausage is previously ground but grind it again after removing casings)*
- ❒ 2 cups chopped ONIONS
- ❒ 5 cloves GARLIC chopped
- ❒ 1 teas SALT
- ❒ 1/4 cup OLIVE OIL
- ❒ 2 - 12 oz cans TOMATO PASTE
- ❒ 2 - cups WATER
- ❒ 3 - 8 oz cans TOMATO SAUCE
- ❒ 2 Tbls Fresh BASIL or 2 teas Dried
- ❒ 2 Tbls Fresh OREGANO or 2 teas Dried
- ❒ 1/2 teas BLACK PEPPER
- ❒ 16 oz GRATED MOZZARELLA CHEESE
- ❒ 15 oz RICOTTA CHEESE
- ❒ 12 oz LASAGNE NOODLES
- ❒ GRATED PARMASAN or ROMANO CHEESE
- ❒ ITALIAN RED SAUCE *(3 oz per serving)*
- ❒ VEGETABLE SPRAY
- ❒ Large pot
- ❒ Chopping board and knife
- ❒ 9 x 13 pan with 2" sides

Method of Preparation

In a large pot sprayed with VEGETABLE SPRAY, saute the following:

- 1/4 cup OLIVE OIL
- 2 lbs GROUND ITALIAN SAUSAGE
- 2 cups chopped ONION
- 5 cloves GARLIC chopped
- 1 teas SALT

THE OLD UNCLE'S ITALIAN SAUSAGE LASAGNE

Continued

Then add:

- 2 - 12 oz cans TOMATO PASTE
- 2 - cups WATER
- 3 - 8 oz cans TOMATO SAUCE
- 2 Tbls Fresh BASIL or 2 teas Dried
- 2 Tbls Fresh OREGANO or 2 teas Dried
- 1/2 teas BLACK PEPPER

Simmer for 2 1/2 hours. Now, do not cook the 12 oz of LASAGNE NOODLES. Simply place them in hot water for about a good minute, then remove. They will remain firm but will be wet.

Spray bottom of 9 x 13 inch pan with 2 inch sides with VEGETABLE SPRAY. Line single layer of the wet noodles on the bottom of the pan.

Now add half of the 16 oz GRATED MOZZARELLA CHEESE. Then comes the RICOTTA CHEESE. Add half of the 15 oz. for the third layer. Now add half of the Meat - Tomato mixture. This completes the first round. Now repeat it, exactly as before starting with the Noodles. If you really like the noodles, add extra ones here. Follow with the other items as before.

When finished the pan should be about full. Now sprinkle the top with GRATED ROMANO or PARMASAN CHEESE. Bake at 335-340 degrees for 45 minutes. Remove from oven and let it cool for about 5 minutes. Now slice it carefully.Add the warmed RED SAUCE on each piece *(Only put a little, maybe 3 oz.)* Sprinkle with GRATED PARMASAN or ROMANO CHEESE and serve.

THE NEPHEW'S FETTUCCINI ALFREDO

Servings - 2

INGREDIENTS & UTENSILS

Turn to the recipe for *The Nephew's Alfredo Sauce.* Follow the recipe listing Ingredients and Utensils .

To the Ingredients, add:

- 9 oz FETTUCCINI PASTA

To the Utensils, add:

- Large Pot to boil Fettuccini
- Pasta Fork

METHOD OF PREPARATION

Boil Fettuccini in a large pot of water with a little salt and olive oil added.

Meanwhile, follow Alfredo Sauce Recipe to make sauce.

Now, stir Fettuccini Pasta as it boils to avoid sticking.As recipe states, reduce cook until Sauce is reduced by 1/3.

Add Noodles to the Sauce, stir well, making sure all noodles get coated with the sauce.

Using a Pasta Fork, ladle the noodles into a pasta bowl. Add about 2 oz of the remaining sauce, and remember, this is not a soup. Be careful not to get too much sauce in the finished product.

You will never eat anything better!

THE NEPHEW'S PASTA POMODORI WITH SHRIMP

INGREDIENTS & UTENSILS

Servings - 4

- ❒ 10 oz ANGEL HAIR PASTA
- ❒ 1 Recipe POMODORI SAUCE
- ❒ 2 Tbls OLIVE OIL
- ❒ 4 cloves Fresh chopped GARLIC
- ❒ 4 Tbls Fresh chopped BASIL
- ❒ 1/2 teas SALT
- ❒ 1/2 teas WHITE PEPPER
- ❒ 16 Large Grilled SHRIMP
- ❒ Large pot to cook pasta
- ❒ Medium saucepan
- ❒ Charcoal Grill

METHOD OF PREPARATION

Make one recipe of POMODORI SAUCE *(q.v.)*

Cook 10 oz ANGEL HAIR PASTA until aldente.

In a saucepan, heat 2 oz OLIVE OIL.
Add:

- 4 cloves Fresh chopped GARLIC
- 4 oz Fresh chopped BASIL.

Saute mixture.

Add:

- 1/2 teas SALT .
- 1/2 teas WHITE PEPPER.

Add 16 Large Grilled SHRIMP and continue to saute.

Now, add POMODORI SAUCE and simmer.

Finally, mix in pasta and serve.

Note - For a light and delicious evening meal.

THE NEPHEW'S CANNELLONI WITH BECHAMEL SAUCE

Servings - 6 This recipe makes 12 stuffed Cannellonis, allowing 2 to a person. The shells measure about 5 inches in length and 1 inch in diameter. An 8 ounce box usually has 14 shells, allowing 2 for breakage, as they are tender once done. Follow directions on the box.

Notes - This recipe is highly recommended, and is not as difficult as it might look like at first. Look it over, this dish can make you the talk of your dinner party. A CLASSIC ITALIAN COOK, no matter what.

Ingredients & Utensils

- ❐ 1 - 8 oz box MANICOTTI or CANNELLONI PASTA
- ❐ 1 lb CHICKEN BREASTS, cut in 3" slices
- ❐ 3 oz *(or 6 Tbls)* CARROTS finely chopped
- ❐ 3 oz *(or 6 Tbls)* ONIONS coarsely chopped
- ❐ 5 oz cleaned SPINACH
- ❐ 2 oz BUTTER or MARGARINE
- ❐ 1/2 teas WHITE PEPPER
- ❐ 1/2 teas CUMIN
- ❐ 1 teas SALT
- ❐ 1/2 cup grated ROMANO CHEESE
- ❐ 1/2 cup RICOTTA CHEESE *(Skim or 1%)*
- ❐ 2 1/2 oz MORTADELLA finely chopped *(Italian Bologna)*
- ❐ One half of 1 EGG, beaten just a little.
- ❐ 1 Recipe BECHAMEL SAUCE *(q.v.)*
- ❐ 6 oz plain ITALIAN RED SAUCE
- ❐ PARSLEY for garnish
- ❐ VEGETABLE SPRAY
- ❐ Medium Saucepan
- ❐ Cutting board and knife
- ❐ 6 Casserole dishes for individual servings. *(If not available, bake in large casserole dish, then transfer to individual platters or plates for servings. Deep dishes do well for the Bechamel Sauce needs to cover as much of the Cannelloni as possible.)*

THE NEPHEW'S CANNELLONI WITH BECHAMEL SAUCE

Continued

METHOD OF PREPARATION

In the Saute pan, melt 2 oz BUTTER or Margarine.

Add:

- 1 lb CHICKEN BREASTS cut into 3" pieces or strips
- 3 oz CARROTS finely chopped
- 3 oz ONIONS coarsely chopped

Cook for about 5 minutes or until done.
Add: 5 oz cleaned *(or frozen)* SPINACH.

Cook for about another 4 minutes, then remove from the heat. Allow to cool.

Transfer to a Cutting Board and chop by hand.

In a large bowl, place chicken and spinach mixture.

Then add:

- 1/2 teas WHITE PEPPER
- 1/2 teas CUMIN
- 1 teas SALT
- 1/2 cup Grated ROMANO CHEESE
- 1/2 cup RICOTTA CHEESE
- 2 1/2 oz MORTADELLA finely chopped
- 1/2 of one EGG slightly beaten

Mix well. Set aside or in the refrigerator.

Boil the MANICOTTI or CANNELLONI SHELLS using directions on the box.

Carefully stuff cooked shells with above mixture.

Continued on the next page following!

THE NEPHEW'S CANNELLONI WITH BECHAMEL SAUCE

Continued

Spray casserole dishes with VEGETABLE SPRAY.

Pour enough warm BECHAMEL SAUCE in the casserole dishes to cover the bottom.

Place cooked stuffed Cannelloni in the dishes. Pour additional Bechamel Sauce in the dishes to about 1/3 of the height of the cannelloni.

Make a small line of ITALIAN RED SAUCE on top of each cannelloni.

Cover loosely with foil, and bake at 350 degrees for 20 minutes. If any of the cannelloni sauce is left, pour over the cannelloni when it is removed from the oven.

Serve and ENJOY!

The Nephew's mother, Rosalie, on steps of the garage apartment where Nash Jr. was born.

THE OLD UNCLE'S SOMETHING SPECIAL

Servings - 2 - A classic new dish that excels in a taste of old Italy. A one of a kind type that adds mushrooms, asparagus, sun-dried tomatoes and spices to a rich cream sauce.

Note— Don't count calories, just enjoy this feast of Italian goodies.

Diet tomorrow!

Ingredients & Utensils

- ❒ VEGETABLE SPRAY
- ❒ 2 oz melted BUTTER or MARGARINE
- ❒ 3 oz MUSHROOMS
- ❒ 3 oz ASPARAGUS
- ❒ 3 oz ARTICHOKE HEARTS
- ❒ 2 oz SUN DRIED TOMATOES
- ❒ 2 Tbls Fresh BASIL or 2 teas Dried
- ❒ 2 Tbls Fresh OREGANO or 2 teas Dried
- ❒ 4 Tbls Grated ROMANO CHEESE
- ❒ 1 teas SALT
- ❒ 1 teas BLACK PEPPER
- ❒ 1 recipe The Old Uncle's VELVET WHITE SAUCE, divided.
- ❒ 10 oz LINGUINI PASTA
- ❒ 2 Saute Pans , medium and small.
- ❒ Large Pot to cook pasta
- ❒ Large spoon, pasta fork
- ❒ Small pan to blanch tomatoes

Method of Preparation

Saute in a Medium Sauce Pan with VEGETABLE SPRAY and 2 oz Melted BUTTER or MARGARINE:

- 3 oz MUSHROOMS
- 3 oz ASPARAGUS
- 3 oz ARTICHOKE HEARTS

Blanch in a small pan of water:

- 2 oz SUN DRIED TOMATOES

Make one recipe of the VELVET WHITE SAUCE. Keep warm. Divide.

In a large pot, cook 10 oz LINGUINI PASTA

Continued on the next page following!

THE OLD UNCLE'S SOMETHING SPECIAL

Continued

in slightly salted water. When done, pour out water, and divide pasta onto two warmed small platters.

Add one half of the warm Velvet White Sauce. Now, arrange the sauteed vegetables and the blanched tomatoes evenly on the platters.

Now sprinkle the 2 Tbls Fresh BASIL and OREGANO evenly on the platters. Then the Blanched 2 oz SUN DRIED TOMATOES can be placed around.

Pour the balance of the Velvet White Sauce on your prize platters. Lastly, add the 3 oz of Grated ROMANO CHEESE as even as possible.

IT'S TIME TO EAT!

The Old Uncle and his wife, Esther Mae, take a moment to share a smile!

THE NEPHEW'S MEZZALUNA

MEZZALUNA STUFFING

Part one of three.

Ingredients & Utensils

- ❒ 1 1/2 lbs cooked CHICKEN finely chopped
- ❒ 1 lb cooked Ground CHICKEN
- ❒ 2 oz LIQUID SMOKE
- ❒ 3 single stalks CELERY finely chopped
- ❒ 1 cup GREEN ONIONS chopped
- ❒ 1 Tbls minced GARLIC
- ❒ 1 teas WHITE PEPPER
- ❒ 1 teas SEASONING SALT
- ❒ 2 Tbls OLIVE OIL
- ❒ 1 cup RICOTTA CHEESE
- ❒ 1 cup ROMANO CHEESE grated
- ❒ Medium Saute Pan
- ❒ Large pot
- ❒ Large Bowl

Method of Preparation

Saute together, then set aside:

- 1 Tbls minced GARLIC
- 3 Single stalks CELERY finely chopped
- 1 cup GREEN ONIONS chopped

Place 1 lb cooked Ground CHICKEN in a small bowl. Pour 2 oz LIQUID SMOKE over the chicken. Set aside.

In a large pot boil water and cook 1 1/2 lbs CHICKEN. After cooking, chop chicken finely or use food processor.

Now, in a large Bowl, mix everything together including the sauteed vegetables, the

Servings - 6 Half moon pasta stuffed with Chicken and Ricotta Cheese in an Alfredo Sauce with Sun dried Tomatoes.

A quote from the Old Uncle: "The shining light recipe in the cooking career of My Nephew. Did you notice he's my Nephew now, replacing my wife."

This recipe takes time, but is easy. We are going to give it to you in three sections: The Stuffing, Making the pasta, and the cooking and Sauce required.

Don't let the three parts scare you away. Once you taste it, you will be very glad you stayed with it. Just ask the Old Uncle.

The Nephew's Mezzaluna is continued on the next two pages!

THE NEPHEW'S MEZZALUNA

Continued

cooked chopped chicken, the cooked Ground Chicken, the one cup of RICOTTA CHEESE, the 1 lb of Grated ROMANO CHEESE, 1 Tbls WHITE PEPPER, 1 Tbls SEASONING SALT, and 2 Tbls OLIVE OIL.

MEZZALUNA PASTA

Part Two of Three.

Servings - 6

Ingredients & Utensils

- ❐ 3 cups FLOUR
- ❐ 2 EGGS
- ❐ 1 cup canned BEETS pureed
- ❐ Mixer and Bowl
- ❐ Rolling Pin
- ❐ 2 1/2 to 3 inch Biscuit Cutter
- ❐ Fork
- ❐ Small Brush *(you also will need a little extra dish of flour and one egg white)*

Method of Preparation

Beat 2 EGGS in a mixing bowl.
Add 3 cups FLOUR gradually along with 1 cup BEETS previously pureed. It should make a stiff dough.

Roll out on a floured board to 1/16 inch thickness. Using a 2 1/2 or 3 inch Biscuit cutter, cut out circles.

Brush half of the circle with egg whites. Now add about 1/2 oz of the Mezzaluna Stuffing. Fold over and seal. Now with a fork, make indent marks along the outside edge.

THE NEPHEW'S MEZZALUNA

THE COOKING AND THE SAUCE FOR *Continued*

MEZZALUNA PASTA

Part Three of Three

INGREDIENTS & UTENSILS

- ❒ All 6 servings of Mezzaluna Pasta previously made.
- ❒ 24 oz HEAVY CREAM
- ❒ 12 oz melted BUTTER
- ❒ 6 oz SUN DRIED TOMATOES
- ❒ 12 oz Grated ROMANO CHEESE
- ❒ Saute Pan
- ❒ Large Pot to boil pasta
- ❒ Pasta Fork
- ❒ Large pot or pan to cook sauce and add pasta.

METHOD OF PREPARATION

Boil all 6 servings of Mezzaluna Pasta until aldente, probably 8 to 10 minutes.

In a separate large pot or pan, put:

- 24 oz HEAVY CREAM
- 12 oz Melted BUTTER
- 6 oz SUN DRIED TOMATOES chopped
- 12 oz Grated ROMANO CHEESE

Mix well and cook to reduce by 1/3.
Add Cooked Pasta and carefully mix until all the pasta is coated with the sauce. Now, divide into six portions, finally adding unused part of the sauce to each serving.

Serve and you will be acclaimed a chef deluxe!

THE OLD UNCLE'S LASAGNE

Servings - 10 An old Italian dish you will never regret making.

INGREDIENTS & UTENSILS

❒ 2 1/2 lbs Ground BEEF
❒ 2 cups chopped ONIONS
❒ 4 cloves chopped GARLIC
❒ 1 teas SALT
❒ 1/4 cup OLIVE OIL
❒ 1 1/2 lbs Fresh TOMATOES chopped
❒ 1 - 12 oz can TOMATO PASTE
❒ 1 - 15 oz can TOMATO SAUCE
❒ 1 - cup WATER
❒ 1 - Tbls Dried BASIL *(or 3 Tbls Fresh)*
❒ 1 - Tbls Dried OREGANO *(or 3 Tbls Fresh)*
❒ 1/2 teas BLACK PEPPER
❒ 16 oz Grated MOZZARELLA CHEESE
❒ 15 oz RICOTTA CHEESE *(May be low fat)*
❒ 12 oz LASAGNE NOODLES
❒ ITALIAN RED SAUCE *(3 oz per serving)*
❒ Grated ROMANO CHEESE for sprinkling
❒ VEGETABLE SPRAY
❒ Chopping board and Knife
❒ Large Pot
❒ 9 x 13 inch Pan with 2 inch sides for cooking Lasagne.

METHOD OF PREPARATION

In a large pot, sprayed with VEGETABLE SPRAY, saute:

- 1/4 cup OLIVE OIL
- 2 1/2 lbs Ground BEEF
- 2 cups chopped ONIONS
- 4 cloves chopped GARLIC
- 1 teas SALT

THE OLD UNCLE'S LASAGNE

Then add:

Continued

- 1 1/2 lbs chopped Fresh TOMATOES
- 1 - 12 oz can TOMATO PASTE
- 1 - 15 oz can TOMATO SAUCE
- 1 - cup WATER
- 1 Tbls Dried BASIL *(or 3 Tbls Fresh)*
- 1 Tbls Dried OREGANO *(or 3 Tbls Fresh)*
- 1/2 teas BLACK PEPPER

Simmer for 2 to 2 1/2 hours. Now, do not cook the 12 oz LASAGNE NOODLES. Simply place them in hot water for a minute or so. They will remain firm but will be wet.

Spray the bottom and sides of a 9 x 13 inch pan with 2 inch sides. Cover the bottom of the pan with a single layer of the wet Lasagne Noodles. Follow with a layer of MOZZARELLA CHEESE *(part skim)*, using half of the 16 oz available. Now comes the RICOTTA CHEESE, using half of the 15 oz available. Now use half of the meat-tomato mixture.

Beginning again with the noodles, repeat each layer as before. When finished, sprinkle with Grated ROMANO CHEESE.

Bake at 335-340 for about 45-50 minutes. Remove from oven, and sprinkle well with the Grated ROMANO CHEESE. Let sit for about 5 minutes or a little more. Then slice and pour about 3 oz of Italian RED SAUCE over each serving. Sprinkle again with the Romano Cheese. Serve and relax. It will be delicious!

THE NEPHEW'S CHEESE RAVIOLI

Servings - 6

Home made Pasta stuffed with a blend of cheeses and sauteed spinach in a red suga sauce. To make this easy and understandable, we are giving this recipe to you in three parts. While it is time consuming, it is worth every minute.

CHEESE RAVIOLI STUFFING

Part one of Three

Ingredients & Utensils

- ❒ 1 lb 6 oz RICCOTTA CHEESE
- ❒ 1/2 EGG
- ❒ 1/4 teas WHITE PEPPER
- ❒ 1/4 cup Chopped PARSLEY
- ❒ 2 cups Grated ROMANO CHEESE
- ❒ 3 1/4 oz Fresh SPINACH, cleaned
- ❒ Medium pot
- ❒ Clean towel
- ❒ Knife
- ❒ Large Mixing Bowl

Method of Preparation

Cook 3 1/4 oz cleaned SPINACH. Drain, then squeeze all water out with a clean towel.

Chop Spinach.

Mix :

- Cooked and chopped Spinach
- 1/2 EGG
- 1/4 teas WHITE PEPPER
- 1/4 cup chopped PARSLEY
- 1 lb 6 oz RICCOTTA CHEESE

Add: 2 cups Grated ROMANO CHEESE a little at a time until desired firmness is attained.

Note - Part one is complete. Now move to Part Two

THE NEPHEW'S CHEESE RAVIOLI

CHEESE RAVIOLI PASTA

Continued

Part Two of Three.

INGREDIENTS & UTENSILS

- ❒ 4 cups All Purpose FLOUR
- ❒ 6 Large EGGS
- ❒ Ravioli Frame and Tray
- ❒ Rolling Pin
- ❒ Sharp Knife
- ❒ Mixing Bowl

Note - You can purchase a Ravioli Frame and Tray at most Wholesale Restaurant Supply Houses. They are inexpensive and helps you make a dozen Ravioli each time. To serve six people, you will need 4 dozen Ravioli.

METHOD OF PREPARATION

In a mixing bowl, place 6 large EGGS and beat slightly. Gradually add 4 cups of All Purpose FLOUR. It should be a stiff dough.

On a floured board, divide and cut dough into four equal parts. Roll out one part at a time to about 1/16th inch thickness. Cut pasta into slightly larger strips than the frame. Lay strip over the frame, make depressions with the tray, fill in stuffing, and cover with the other piece of dough, stretching it to completely cover frame.

Now use rolling pin to press down and seal ravioli. Repeat with the other three pieces of dough. Makes four dozen Ravioli.

Part Two is complete. Move to Part Three

THE NEPHEW'S CHEESE RAVIOLI

Continued

CHEESE RAVIOLI

COOKING AND SAUCE

Part Three of Three

INGREDIENTS & UTENSILS

- ❒ All Six servings of the CHEESE RAVIOLI *(48 Ravioli in all)*
- ❒ 15 oz ITALIAN SUGA SAUCE *(If you have any available, use The Nephews Suga Sauce or the Old Uncle's Italian Red Sauce.)*
- ❒ 2 Tbls Grated ROMANO CHEESE
- ❒ Saute Pan to warm Sauce
- ❒ Pot to cook Ravioli
- ❒ Serving dishes

METHOD OF PREPARATION

Cook Ravioli in boiling water.

Pour warmed Suga Sauce over Ravioli. Put in individual plates and sprinkle Grated Romano Cheese over the ravioli and suga sauce. Wonderful eating!

The Nephew and his daughter, Brina, inside D'Amico Italian Café.

The Nephew (foreground) with big brother, Frank and little sister, Paula Jean.

THE NEPHEW'S MEAT RAVIOLI

MEAT RAVIOLI STUFFING

Part One of three

INGREDIENTS & UTENSILS

- ❒ 1 3/4 lbs lean Ground BEEF
- ❒ 1/2 cup CARROTS, finely chopped
- ❒ 6 individual stalks CELERY, finely chopped
- ❒ 2 individual SHALLOTS, finely chopped
- ❒ 1/4 Medium ONION, finely chopped
- ❒ 4 cloves GARLIC, finely chopped
- ❒ 1 cup SUGA SAUCE
- ❒ 1/3 cup BEEF STOCK
- ❒ 1/8 teas WHITE PEPPER
- ❒ 1 Tbls SALT
- ❒ 2 Tbls VEGETABLE OIL
- ❒ Chopping Board, Knife or Food Processor
- ❒ Large Pot

METHOD OF PREPARATION

Heat VEGETABLE OIL in a large pot.

Add:

- 1/2 cup CARROTS
- 6 stalks CELERY
- 2 SHALLOTS
- 1/4 Medium ONION
- 4 cloves GARLIC

Saute for about 5 minutes.

Add: 1 3/4 lbs Ground BEEF, and saute until completely done.

Drain off all excess grease.

Servings - 6

As with the Mezzaluna and Cheese Ravioli Recipes, we are going to give this to you in three parts. While it may be time consuming, I guarantee the return is worth it. Delicious to eat, and a sense of pride in your cooking. Some people brag about being lazy and not cooking. I would think they could find something else to brag about.

Go ahead and make this recipe. Be a great cook. It's easy.

THE NEPHEW'S MEAT RAVIOLI

Continued

Add:

- 1 cup SUGA SAUCE
- 1/3 cup BEEF STOCK
- 1/8 teas WHITE PEPPER
- 1 Tbls SALT

Cook over Medium Heat for about 1/2 hour.
Part one is complete. Now move to Part two.

Note- You can purchase a Ravioli Frame and Tray at most Wholesale Restaurant Supply Houses. They are inexpensive. With these, you cut out and make a dozen Ravioli at a time. You will need 4 Dozen to serve 6 people.

MAKING THE RAVIOLI

Part Two of Three.

Ingredients & Utensils

❒ 4 cups FLOUR
❒ 6 Large EGGS
❒ Ravioli Frame and Tray
❒ Rolling Pin
❒ Sharp Knife
❒ Mixing Bowl

Method of Preparation

In a large mixing bowl, place 6 large EGGS and slightly beat them. Slowly add 4 cups of FLOUR gradually until desired firmness is obtained. It might take slightly more or less flour.

On a floured board, divide and cut dough into four equal parts. Roll out one part at a time. It should be about 1/16 inches thick Make two strips shaped like the Ravioli Tray, only slightly larger. Now lay one strip over the frame, and use the tray to make depressions in the dough. Place stuffing into the depressions. Then lay the other strip on top. Now, with

THE NEPHEW'S MEAT RAVIOLI

Continued

the rolling pin, carefully press down as you roll it over the dough and frame. This will seal and cut out the dozen ravioli. Now proceed with the next piece of dough.

When the four dozen ravioli are completed, you are finished with Part Two. Now move to Part Three

MEAT RAVIOLI

COOKING AND SAUCE

Part Three of Three

INGREDIENTS & UTENSILS

- ❒ 48 - Meat Ravioli *(Prepared in Part Two)*
- ❒ 6 oz SUGA SAUCE *(The Nephew's Suga Sauce or The Old Uncle's Italian Red Sauce or Plain Red Sauce from the Store)*
- ❒ 3 Tbls Grated ROMANO CHEESE
- ❒ Large Pot to cook Ravioli
- ❒ Sauce Pan to warm Suga Sauce
- ❒ Pasta Fork

Grandmother Jennie D'Amico, with sons Sam and Nash, Sr. and daughter, Esther Mae

METHOD OF PREPARATION

Cook 48 RAVIOLI in Large Pot in boiling water until aldente.

Warm 6 oz SUGA SAUCE in sauce pan until heated. Put 8 hot Ravioli in each of the small platters or dishes.

Pour hot SUGA SAUCE over the Ravioli, tossing to cover well.

Line up Ravioli, with four on each side.

Sprinkle with 3 Tbls Grated ROMANO CHEESE and serve. Enjoy!

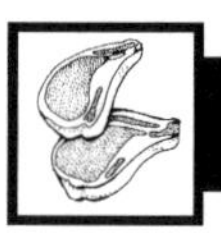

PART THREE: MEAT DISHES

Chicken - Veal -Wild Game

THE NEPHEW AND THE OLD UNCLE sat at their favorite spot in the patio at the D'AMICO ITALIAN MARKET CAFE. It was a Friday afternoon, and the walking traffic was terrific and interesting.

"Tell me, Old Uncle, about the Meat Dishes you have planned for our new book?"

"Well now, let me think."

At this point , the Nephew interrupted. "Don't give me none of that funny business like in the pasta section."

The Old Uncle laughed. "Sometimes, I don't think you trust the best Uncle you ever had."

"Get to the Meat Dishes."

"OK, OK. I am taking two of my outstanding recipes from my HUNT 'EM CATCH 'EM AND COOK 'EM Book, and converting them into Chicken Recipes. I also plan to do something similar when we get to the seafood section."

"Sounds great. Mine are mostly mixed between our other book and recipes off our menu."

The Nephew laughed. The Old Uncle smiled just a little.

"You better hope you even make it to eighty. Ask my sweet wife sometimes. She won't tell you a thing but she might give you a telling smile."

"You old rascal, I love you even if I can't get the best of you."

THE NEPHEW'S CHICKEN PICCATA

Servings - 2

Sauteed Chicken Breast in sauce consisting of Lemon, Butter, White Wine, and Artichoke Hearts.

Ingredients & Utensils

- ❒ 2 - 8 oz Boneless Skinless CHICKEN BREASTS, slightly pounded
- ❒ 4 canned ARTICHOKE HEARTS, sliced
- ❒ 6 oz WHITE WINE
- ❒ 4 oz STOCK *(use 1/2 teas Chicken Bouillon and 4 oz water)*
- ❒ 1 1/2 cups flour, for dredging
- ❒ 4 oz BUTTER
- ❒ 1 whole Fresh Lemon
- ❒ 4 oz OLIVE OIL
- ❒ Medium Saute Pan
- ❒ Plate for dredging chicken breasts
- ❒ Measuring utensils

Method of Preparation

Heat 4 oz OLIVE OIL in saute pan. Using 1 1/2 cups FLOUR, dredge 2 boneless skinless CHICKEN BREASTS. Saute until golden brown on both sides.

Add 6 oz WHITE WINE and 4 oz STOCK

Then add: 4 each canned ARTICHOKE HEARTS and 4 oz BUTTER

Now Squeeze whole fresh LEMON, and cook until reduced by about 1/3.

Serve and Enjoy.

THE NEPHEW'S CHICKEN MOSTARDA

Breaded Chicken Breasts in a rich creamy mustard sauce.

Servings - 4

INGREDIENTS & UTENSILS

❒ 8 - 4 oz CHICKEN BREASTS *(2 whole chicken breasts, each one divided and then cut in half)*
❒ SALT and PEPPER for seasoning
❒ 2 EGGS, slightly beaten, for egg wash
❒ PLAIN BREAD CRUMBS for dredging
❒ 1 Recipe THE NEPHEW'S MOSTARDA SAUCE
❒ Small Dishes for Egg and Bread Crumbs
❒ Large Saute Pan
❒ Bowl or pan to warm sauce.

METHOD OF PREPARATION

Make one Recipe of the MOSTARDA SAUCE Recipe. Set it aside.

Sprinkle the 8 - 4 oz pieces of Chicken BREASTS with the SALT and PEPPER.

Now dip the Chicken pieces in a small bowl containing 2 beaten EGGS. Coat them well.

Next, dredge the Chicken pieces in a small dish containing PLAIN BREAD CRUMBS.

Now, saute in VEGETABLE SPRAY and 1 oz OLIVE OIL on both sides until done.

Meanwhile warm the Mostarda Sauce, and pour over the Chicken pieces in individual serving dishes. *(Two pieces per person).*

ENJOY!

THE OLD UNCLE'S ITALIAN SEASONED CHICKEN CASSEROLE

INGREDIENTS & UTENSILS

Servings - ?

- ❒ 2 CHICKENS, cut into regular serving pieces *(See Notes)*
- ❒ 1 APPLE, 1 ONION, and 1 single stalk CELERY, all quartered
- ❒ 2 Tbls GARLIC POWDER
- ❒ BLACK PEPPER for sprinkling
- ❒ VEGETABLE SPRAY
- ❒ 1 Pkg. LASAGNE NOODLES
- ❒ VEGETABLE SPRAY
- ❒ 1 Medium ONION, finely chopped
- ❒ 6 cloves GARLIC, finely chopped
- ❒ 1 Large BELL PEPPER or 2 medium, cleaned, and finely chopped
- ❒ 1 JALAPENO, cleaned and finely chopped
- ❒ 1 can CREAM OF MUSHROOM SOUP
- ❒ 1 can CREAM OF CELERY SOUP
- ❒ 1 14 1/2 oz can CRUSHED TOMATOES
- ❒ 1/2 cup Grated ROMANO CHEESE
- ❒ 1 Tbls CHILI POWDER
- ❒ 1 teas SALT
- ❒ 3 Large or 6 Medium Fresh TOMATOES, cut in bite size pieces
- ❒ 12 oz Shredded MOZZARELLA CHEESE
- ❒ Large Pot with Top
- ❒ Chopping board and knife
- ❒ Skillet to saute in
- ❒ Large bowl
- ❒ Large casserole Dish
- ❒ Large spoon

Notes - If you prefer to use Chicken Breasts, it would take about 4 lbs. Actually this recipe could be made with almost any kind of bird. This recipe is similar to The Old Uncle's Mexican Seasoned Wild Turkey Recipe in the HUNT 'EM CATCH 'EM and COOK 'EM Book written and published by The Old Uncle in 1999.

THE OLD UNCLE'S ITALIAN SEASONED CHICKEN CASSEROLE

Continued

METHOD OF PREPARATION

In a large Pot almost filled with water, place:

- 2 cut up CHICKENS
- 1 APPLE, 1 ONION, and 1 single stalk of CELERY, all quartered.

Toss 2 Tbls GARLIC POWDER over the mixture, and finally sprinkle with BLACK PEPPER. Keep on medium heat until it boils. Reduce heat and simmer for several hours until tender. *(about 2 hours)*

Warm some water, and place the LASAGNE NOODLES in it. Do not cook the noodles, just leave them in the hot water for a minute or so. They will remain firm, but will be wet. Now fit them into a large casserole dish, previously sprayed with VEGETABLE SPRAY. *(single layer)*

When Chickens are tender, remove, and cut into bite size pieces. Discard the bones and the ingredients used to flavor the chickens. Set Chicken meat aside or in the refrigerator.

Spray a skillet with VEGETABLE SPRAY. Add:

- 1 Tbls Olive Oil
- 1 Medium ONION, finely chopped
- 6 cloves GARLIC, finely chopped
- 1 Large BELL PEPPER or 2 medium cleaned and finely chopped
- 1 JALAPENO, cleaned and finely chopped

THE OLD UNCLE'S ITALIAN SEASONED CHICKEN CASSEROLE

Continued

Saute until soft. *(about 5 minutes)*

Place in a large bowl, and add:

- 1 can CREAM OF MUSHROOM SOUP
- 1 can CREAM OF CELERY SOUP
- 1- 14 1/2 oz can CRUSHED TOMATOES
- 1/2 cup Grated ROMANO CHEESE
- 1 Tbls CHILI POWDER
- 1 teas SALT

Mix well. Set aside.

Now chop into small or bite size pieces, 3 Large or 6 small Fresh TOMATOES.

Then combine the Chicken with the sauteed vegetable and soup mixture. Mix well with a large spoon.

Place half of the above mixture on top of the noodles in the large casserole dish. Smooth it out.Add one half of the chopped fresh tomatoes.

Follow this with one half of the 12 oz SHREDDED MOZZARELLA CHEESE.

Now, start over, beginning with the Lasagne Noodles. Place them in a single layer.

Follow this with the other mixtures, same order as before.

Bake at 375 degrees for 35 - 40 minutes until steaming hot.

Serve and enjoy. The master chef has done it again

THE NEPHEW'S CHICKEN CUSCINETTI

Servings - 2

Note - Serve something that does not overpower the delicate taste of the delicious cuscinetti.

INGREDIENTS & UTENSILS

- ❒ 2-8 oz CHICKEN BREASTS *(Breasts of one chicken)* Skinless and Pounded Flat.
- ❒ 2 - 2 oz Pieces PROSCUITTO *(Italian Ham)*
- ❒ 2 - 2 oz Slices MOZZARELLA CHEESE
- ❒ FLOUR for dredging
- ❒ 2 EGGS Slightly beaten for Dredging
- ❒ 2 -Tbls OLIVE OIL
- ❒ 6 oz MARSALA WINE *(sweet type)*
- ❒ 4 oz ITALIAN SUGA SAUCE or RED SAUCE
- ❒ 3 oz BUTTER or MARGARINE
- ❒ VEGETABLE SPRAY
- ❒ 2 small bowls for dredging
- ❒ 9 inch saute pan
- ❒ Medium Casserole dish with top

METHOD OF PREPARATION

Skin and pound flat 2 -8 oz CHICKEN BREASTS *(Breasts of one chicken)*

To each piece add:

- 1 - 2 oz slice PROSCUITTO *(Italian ham)*
- 1 - 2 oz slice MOZZARELLA CHEESE

Fold each piece over, forming a sandwich effect. Secure with a toothpick.

Dredge each cuscinetti in the FLOUR. Follow this, by dredging the cuscinettis in the 2 EGGS, that have been slightly beaten.

Spray a 9 inch saute pan with VEGETABLE SPRAY. Add 2 oz OLIVE OIL and brown the cusinettis on both sides.

THE NEPHEW'S CHICKEN CUSCINETTI

Continued

Place in the Casserole Dish both of the cusinettis. Cover, and bake at 350 degrees for 30 minutes.

Meanwhile, slowly prepare the sauce.

Discard oil in the saute pan.

Add
- 6 oz MARSALA WINE
- 4 oz ITALIAN SUGA SAUCE or RED SAUCE.

Cook on low heat, stirring occasionally until reduced to half.

Add 3 oz BUTTER. Stir occasionally.

Warm over low heat, then pour over the cusinettis and ENJOY!

Chicken Cuscinetti

THE OLD UNCLE'S MUSHROOM CHICKEN

Servings - 4

INGREDIENTS & UTENSILS

❒ 4 - 8 oz CHICKEN BREASTS, skinless and boneless *(The breasts of 2 chickens)*
❒ VEGETABLE SPRAY
❒ 2 Tbls melted BUTTER
❒ 1 - 10 1/2 oz can CREAM OF MUSHROOM SOUP, fat reduced
❒ 1 - 10 1/2 oz can CREAM OF CELERY SOUP, fat reduced
❒ 1 1/2 cups WHITE WINE
❒ 2 teas Dried Basil or 2 Tbls Fresh
❒ 2 teas Dried OREGANO or 2 Tbls Fresh
❒ 1 teas Dried ROSEMARY or 1 Tbls Fresh
❒ 1/2 teas Ground BLACK PEPPER
❒ 1/2 teas RED PEPPER Ground or Flakes
❒ 8 oz Small Fresh MUSHROOMS
❒ Large Saute pan
❒ Casserole Dish *(10 x 10 x 2)*
❒ Large Bowl and spoon
❒ Large Spoon
❒ Aluminum Foil to cover casserole

METHOD OF PREPARATION

In a large skillet, previously sprayed with VEGETABLE SPRAY, place 2 Tbls melted BUTTER. Then add the 4 - 8 oz skinless, boneless CHICKEN BREASTS. Brown the chicken pieces, and transfer to a casserole dish *(10 x 10 x 2).*

 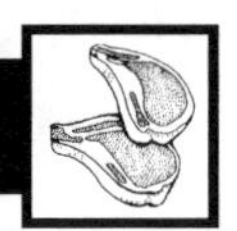

THE OLD UNCLE'S MUSHROOM CHICKEN

Continued

In a large bowl, add and mix well:

- 1-10 1/2 oz can CREAM OF MUSHROOM SOUP, fat reduced
- 1 - 10 1/2 oz can CREAM OF CELERY SOUP, fat reduced
- 1 1/2 cups WHITE WINE
- 2 teas Dried BASIL or 2 Tbls Fresh
- 2 teas Dried OREGANO or 2 Tbls Fresh
- 1 teas Dried ROSEMARY or 1 Tbls Fresh
- 1/2 teas Ground BLACK PEPPER
- 1/2 teas RED PEPPER, Ground or Flakes

With a large spoon, carefully cover each of the Chicken Breasts.

Then add the 8 oz of Small Fresh Mushrooms on top.

Carefully seal the casserole dish with a piece of ALUMINUM FOIL. Be sure it's sealed well.

Cook at 350 degrees for one hour and fifteen minutes.
Remove from oven and check for tenderness. If not tender, seal up the casserole again with the foil, and let it cook another thirty minutes. It should be ready for sure, at that time.

Remove from casserole. Serve with the juices in the casserole dish. Guaranteed to be delicious.

The Old Uncle as a young boy.

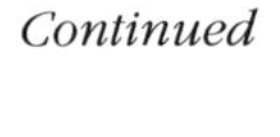

THE NEPHEW'S CHICKEN PRIMAVERA WITH BECHAMEL SAUCE

Servings - 6

Ingredients & Utensils

For CHICKEN:

- ❒ 6 CHICKEN BREASTS
- ❒ 12 oz RICOTTA CHEESE
- ❒ 3 oz each of CELERY, ONIONS, and CARROTS, all diced
- ❒ 8 oz all purpose FLOUR
- ❒ 8 oz OLIVE OIL
- ❒ 10 WHOLE EGGS
- ❒ 1 1/2 cups grated ROMANO CHEESE

For BECHAMEL SAUCE:

- ❒ 1/2 ONION, diced
- ❒ 2 BAY LEAVES
- ❒ 1 teas NUTMEG
- ❒ 1 teas WHITE PEPPER
- ❒ 1 teas SALT
- ❒ 6 oz MILK
- ❒ 3 oz All purpose FLOUR
- ❒ 4 oz UNSALTED BUTTER
- ❒ Knife and chopping board
- ❒ Pieces of plastic wrap
- ❒ Large Mixing Board
- ❒ Mallet
- ❒ Dishes for dredging
- ❒ Frying Pan
- ❒ Large Saute Pan
- ❒ Strainer and Large Pot

Method of Preparation

For CHICKEN:

Cut each of the 6 CHICKEN BREASTS in half. Pound each piece between plastic wrap with a mallet.

THE NEPHEW'S CHICKEN PRIMAVERA WITH BECHAMEL SAUCE

Continued

Place 3 oz of each *(previously diced)* CELERY, ONION, and CARROTS in a large mixing bowl. Add 12 oz RICOTTA CHEESE and 1 1/2 cups Grated ROMANO CHEESE. Mix well.

Lay out all the Chicken Pieces, and spread about an ounce of mixture over each. Roll up each piece of Chicken.

In a bowl, lightly beat 10 WHOLE EGGS. Place in a bowl for dredging. In another bowl, put the 8 oz All Purpose FLOUR. Now dredge the Chicken pieces in flour first, then in the Eggs, and again in the flour. In a large skillet, fry Chicken pieces in 8 oz OLIVE OIL until crust is golden brown. Finally, cook chicken on low heat until well done.

For BECHAMEL SAUCE:
In a large saute pan, saute 1/2 ONION diced, 2 BAY LEAVES, 1 teas NUTMEG, 1 teas WHITE PEPPER, and 1 teas SALT. Slowly add 6 oz MILK being careful not to scald. Gradually add 4 oz FLOUR, and the 3 oz BUTTER. Now, if the Sauce is too watery, add a little flour. If too thick, add water. It should have the consistency of a creamy soup. When satisfied, remove from the heat. Pour the sauce over a fine mesh strainer held over a large pot. This will eliminate the whole pieces of onion and other spices.

Place two rolled chicken pieces on each plate, and top with Sauce.

Enjoy!

THE NEPHEW'S CHICKEN ROMANO

Servings - 6

Note- Easy and delicious. If you don't have the Suga or Red Sauce, buy a bottle at the grocery store

INGREDIENTS & UTENSILS

❒ 6 CHICKEN BREASTS, 6 oz each
❒ 6 oz PROSCIUTTO, chopped
❒ 8 oz BUTTON MUSHROOMS, sliced
❒ 6 oz GREEN PEAS
❒ 16 oz MARSALA WINE, dry type
❒ 6 oz UNSALTED BUTTER
❒ 10 oz ITALIAN SUGA or RED SAUCE
❒ 6 oz OLIVE OIL
❒ 1 teas SALT
❒ 1 teas BLACK PEPPER
❒ 1 teas WHITE PEPPER
❒ FLOUR
❒ Large Saute Pan or Large Skillet
❒ Chopping Board and Knife

METHOD OF PREPARATION

Lightly flour 6 CHICKEN BREASTS. In a Large hot saute pan, add 6 oz OLIVE OIL. Saute Chicken Breasts until golden brown on both sides.

Add:

- 6 oz chopped PROSCIUTTO
- 8 oz BUTTON MUSHROOMS
- 16 oz dry MARSALA WINE
- 6 oz UNSALTED BUTTER

Simmer until all ingredients are incorporated.

Then add

- 10 oz ITALIAN SUGA or RED SAUCE
- 6 oz GREEN PEAS
- 1 teas SALT
- 1 teas BLACK PEPPER
- 1 teas WHITE PEPPER

Simmer until Chicken is thoroughly cooked.

THE NEPHEW'S CHICKEN BRACIOLENTINI

INGREDIENTS & UTENSILS

Servings - 4

- ❒ 4 pieces CHICKEN BREASTS *(the breasts of two chickens)*
- ❒ 1/2 lb ITALIAN SAUSAGE *(with casings removed)*
- ❒ 2 Tbls OLIVE OIL
- ❒ 1/2 cup ONION, finely chopped
- ❒ 1 clove GARLIC, chopped
- ❒ 3 oz cleaned SPINACH, fresh or frozen
- ❒ 1/2 cup Grated ROMANO CHEESE
- ❒ 1/4 cup Italian Seasoned BREAD CRUMBS
- ❒ SALT and PEPPER to taste
- ❒ FLOUR for dredging
- ❒ 4 WHOLE EGGS
- ❒ 3 Tbls OLIVE OIL
- ❒ 5 oz CHICKEN BROTH or STOCK
- ❒ 5 oz WHITE WINE
- ❒ 4 oz BUTTER
- ❒ Clever or Mallet with Chopping Board to pound Chicken
- ❒ 12 inch Pan or Electric Skillet to saute Sausage and other items
- ❒ Sharp Knife, Mixing Bowl, and Toothpicks
- ❒ 2 bowls for dredging flour and eggs

METHOD OF PREPARATION

With a mallet, pound the 4 pieces of CHICKEN BREASTS *(2 whole chicken breasts divided)* Set aside.

THE NEPHEW'S CHICKEN BRACIOLENTINI

Continued

Saute in a pan over medium to low heat:
- 1/2 lb ITALIAN SAUSAGE until done. *(in bulk form with casings removed)*

Drain, discarding the fat,

Saute in 2 oz OLIVE OIL:
- 1/2 cup finely chopped ONIONS
- 1 chopped clove GARLIC

Until Onions are translucent.

Add 3 oz chopped SPINACH, and saute for 2 or 3 minutes Remove from pan, and place on a cutting board. Now, chop coarsely by hand. Add Sausage and Spinach mixtures to the mixing bowl.

Add:
- 1/2 cup Grated ROMANO CHEESE
- 1/4 cup Italian Seasoned BREAD CRUMBS

Mix well, adding SALT and PEPPER to taste. Now, cool completely.

Place about 3 Tbls of Stuffing Mixture in the center of each flattened Chicken Breast. Fold the ends in about a 1/2 inch, then roll until the sides meet. Secure with a toothpick or two. At this point, you may

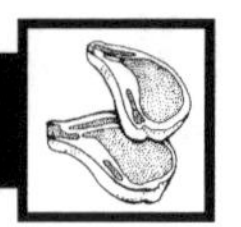

THE NEPHEW'S CHICKEN BRACIOLENTINI

Continued

cook to finish, or refrigerate until later.

Dredge the Wrapped Chicken Pieces in FLOUR, then in beaten WHOLE EGGS. Add 3 oz OLIVE Oil to a pan or electric skillet. When hot, add the rolled Chicken pieces, and cook until brown all around. Now remove the oil from the pan.

Add:
- 5 oz CHICKEN STOCK
- 5 oz WHITE WINE

Cook until reduced by 1/2.

Add 4 oz BUTTER

Cook until sauce is well blended with the butter. Remove from fire, pour sauce over the Chicken Braciolentini, and Serve.

Chicken Braciolentini

THE NEPHEW'S VEAL SALTIMBOCCA

Servings - 6

Ingredients & Utensils

- ❒ 12 small VEAL CUTLETS, 2 oz each, thin
- ❒ 7 oz OLIVE OIL
- ❒ 6 oz PROSCIUTTO
- ❒ 6 oz MOZZARELLA CHEESE, sliced
- ❒ 12 Fresh SAGE LEAVES, chopped or 1 Tbls Dried
- ❒ 24 oz MARSALA WINE
- ❒ 8 oz BUTTON MUSHROOMS
- ❒ 8 oz Fresh SPINACH
- ❒ 4 oz UNSALTED BUTTER
- ❒ 4 WHOLE EGGS
- ❒ 1 teas SALT
- ❒ 1 teas WHITE PEPPER
- ❒ 1 teas BLACK PEPPER
- ❒ All Purpose FLOUR
- ❒ Mallet and chopping board
- ❒ Plastic wrap
- ❒ 2 bowls for dredging
- ❒ Large Saute Skillet
- ❒ Skillet and toothpicks

Method of Preparation

Pound all 12 VEAL CUTLETS between 2 pieces of plastic wrap until 1/4 inch thick.

Lay out all Cutlets and place 1 slice of PROSCIUTTO and MOZZARELLA on each one. Roll each piece and secure with toothpicks.

Slightly beat 4 WHOLE EGGS, place in a small dish. Dredge Cutlets in FLOUR, then in EGGS, and again in Flour.

THE NEPHEW'S VEAL SALTIMBOCCA

Continued

In a hot skillet, saute Cutlets until lightly browned.

Add:

- 8 oz sliced BUTTON MUSHROOMS
- 24 oz MARSALA WINE
- 12 SAGE LEAVES, chopped
- 4 oz UNSALTED BUTTER
- 1 Teas each of SALT, WHITE PEPPER and BLACK PEPPER

Simmer until all ingredients are well incorporated in the sauce.

While dish is simmering, in 2 remaining oz of OLIVE OIL, saute 8 oz Fresh SPINACH until slightly wilted.

Divide SPINACH on the 6 platters, top with two Cutlets and sauce on each platter or large dish. ENJOY!

Veal Saltimbocca

THE NEPHEW'S OSSO BUCO

Servings - 6

Veal Shank: The closer to the bone, the sweeter the meat!

INGREDIENTS & UTENSILS

- ❒ 6 VEAL SHANKS, 3 inches thick
- ❒ 3 YELLOW SQUASH
- ❒ 3 ZUCCHINI
- ❒ 3 CARROTS
- ❒ 3 small ONIONS
- ❒ 1 1/2 Bunches of CELERY
- ❒ zest of one LEMON
- ❒ 2 Qts CRUSHED TOMATOES, with JUICE
- ❒ 1 cup WHITE WINE
- ❒ 1 cup RED WINE
- ❒ 1 teas WHITE PEPPER
- ❒ 1 teas BLACK PEPPER
- ❒ 1 teas SALT
- ❒ 1 teas crushed GARLIC
- ❒ 2 teas OLIVE OIL
- ❒ All PURPOSE FLOUR
- ❒ Chopping Board and Sharp Knife
- ❒ Dish for dredging
- ❒ Skillet
- ❒ Large Saute Pan
- ❒ Deep Casserole Dish with Lid

METHOD OF PREPARATION

Finely Dice:

- 3 Yellow Squash
- 3 ZUCCHINI
- 3 CARROTS
- 3 small ONIONS
- 1 1/2 Bunches of CELERY

Lightly dredge 6 VEAL SHANKS in FLOUR, and braise in a hot skillet. Set aside.

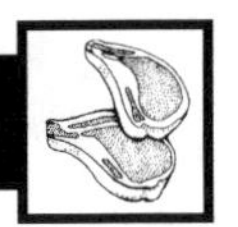

THE NEPHEW'S OSSO BUCO

Continued

In a hot skillet, saute all the above diced vegetables until aldente.

In a heavy saute pan, add 2 teas OLIVE OIL. Add:

- Zest of one lemon
- 2 quarts of CRUSHED TOMATOES with SAUCE
- 1 cup WHITE WINE
- 1 cup RED WINE
- 3 oz BEEF STOCK
- 1 teas WHITE PEPPER
- 1 teas BLACK PEPPER
- 1 teas SALT
- 1 teas chopped GARLIC

Simmer sauce mixture well.

In a deep casserole dish with a lid, place the 6 Braised Veal Shanks. Top with the Vegetable mixture and the sauce.

Cook covered at 375 degrees for 60 - 75 minutes. Serve and ENJOY!

Osso Buco

THE NEPHEW'S VEAL ALLA MILANESE

Servings - 6

INGREDIENTS & UTENSILS

- ❒ 6 VEAL CUTLETS, 4 oz each
- ❒ 4 Italian seasoned BREAD CRUMBS
- ❒ 2 cups All Purpose FLOUR
- ❒ 6 WHOLE EGGS
- ❒ 6 oz OLIVE OIL
- ❒ 6 LEMON WEDGES
- ❒ PARSLEY SPRIG
- ❒ Plastic wrap
- ❒ Mallet
- ❒ Chopping board
- ❒ 3 Bowls for dredging
- ❒ Small skillet

METHOD OF PREPARATION

Place all 6 VEAL CUTLETS between two pieces of plastic wrap, and pound with a mallet on your chopping block until they are about 1/4 inch thick.

Beat 6 WHOLE EGGS in a bowl and set aside.

Dredge pounded Veal in 2 cups FLOUR, then in beaten Eggs, and finally in 4 oz Italian seasoned BREAD CRUMBS. *(Be sure to coat each cutlet evenly as you move from bowl to bowl.)*

In a hot skillet, place 1 oz of OLIVE OIL and heat. Place one cutlet at a time, and cook until golden brown. Then, starting with another cutlet, place 1 more oz of Olive Oil, and repeat as before. Repeat.

When finished, put each cutlet on a 9 inch plate, add a LEMON WEDGE, and a sprig of PARSLEY. Enjoy!

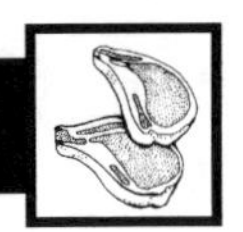

THE OLD UNCLE'S DREAM CREAMED QUAIL ITALIAN STYLE

INGREDIENTS & UTENSILS

Servings - 4

- ❒ 8 QUAIL, picked
- ❒ VEGETABLE SPRAY
- ❒ 2 Tbls BUTTER
- ❒ 1 10 1/2 oz can CREAM OF MUSHROOM SOUP reduced fat
- ❒ 1 10 1/2 oz can CREAM OF CELERY SOUP reduced fat
- ❒ 1 1/2 cups WHITE WINE
- ❒ 2 Tbls Fresh BASIL or 2 teas dried
- ❒ 1 Tbls Fresh OREGANO or 1 teas dried
- ❒ 1 Tbls Fresh ROSEMARY or 1 teas dried
- ❒ 1 teas BLACK PEPPER
- ❒ 1/2 teas crushed RED PEPPER
- ❒ 2 oz AMARETTO or STREGA LIQUEUR
- ❒ Large skillet
- ❒ Large casserole dish
- ❒ Spoon for basting
- ❒ Large Bowl and Fork
- ❒ Aluminum foil

Notes - The Amaretto would add extra sweetness, while the Strega is more potent.

If the recipe makes your mouth water, and you don't have any quail, you could substitute a cut up 3 1/2 or 4 lb Chicken, or you could use some other game bird like doves

METHOD OF PREPARATION

In a large skillet sprayed with VEGETABLE SPRAY, add 2 oz BUTTER. When melted, add the 8 QUAIL and brown them well.

Transfer the birds to a Large Casserole Dish sprayed with Vegetable Spray. Lay the birds breast side up.

The Old Uncle's Dream Creamed Quail Italian Style is continued on the next page following!

THE OLD UNCLE'S DREAM CREAMED QUAIL ITALIAN STYLE

Continued

In a large bowl, add and mix well:

- 1 10 1/2 oz can CREAM OF MUSHROOM SOUP reduced fat
- 1 10 1/2 oz can CREAM OF CELERY SOUP reduced fat
- 1 1/2 cups WHITE WINE
- 2 Tbls Fresh BASIL or 2 teas dried
- 1 Tbls Fresh OREGANO or 1 teas dried
- 1 Tbls Fresh ROSEMARY or 1 teas dried
- 1 teas BLACK PEPPER
- 1/2 teas crushed RED PEPPER
- 2 oz AMARETTO or STREGA LIQUEUR

Carefully cover the Quail with the mixture.

Set the oven at 325 degrees. Seal the birds in the casserole dish with ALUMINUM FOIL.

Now, place in the oven and bake for an hour. Check for doneness, and if it's not ready, you have to reseal the foil again. Cook another 20 or 30 minutes.

When ready, pour the pan juices over the birds, and serve. You have my personal guarantee on this one. It's delicious

The Old Uncle keeps a keen eye on his retrievers. He raised, trained and judged retrievers for 30 years.

THE OLD UNCLE'S DOVES WITH ITALIAN SAUCE AND PASTA

Ingredients and Method of Preparation

Servings - 6

My Italian Taste Buds tell me this is the finest dish in the book !

Make one recipe of The Old Uncle's Italian Red Sauce. (q.v.) During the first hour while the sauce is simmering, brown 12 DOVES, picked or skinned, preferably whole birds, but if you just have the breasts, they will suffice.

You can either brown them in a skillet with VEGETABLE SPRAY and 2-3 Tbls of OLIVE OIL as needed, or a healthier way would be to put them on a flat pan, sprayed with Vegetable Spray, and bake in the oven only until they are slightly browned. *(350 Degrees)*

After one hour, add the browned doves to the Sauce. Continue to simmer for three more hours.

At the conclusion of this time, check the sauce for flavor, you might need more salt, pepper or another spice .

Satisfied with the sauce, now check the doves. They should be tender, but just be sure. If you find a tough one or two, take the others out and cook the sauce longer with the tough doves until they are tender.

A little trouble, yes, but worth every minute, I promise you. The sauce will have a flavor like you won't believe.

You know you are a chef, so stick out your chest and enjoy your masterpiece.

PART FOUR: SEAFOOD DISHES

Fish - Shrimp - Crab

The Nephew and the Old Uncle motored down toward Galveston. The Old Uncle was recovering from a heart problem that almost cashed in his chips.

"Nephew, tell me about your Italian seafood dishes that will be representing the restaurant in our new cookbook."

It didn't take the Nephew long to reply.

"Old Uncle, why don't we hear about your plans first this time?"

The Nephew glanced away from the highway for just a second. A smile spread across his face.

"What's the matter, Old Man. You afraid I might scoop you this time.?"

"I love you, Nephew. Fear is not in my body for any reason. You little whippersnapper, you may think you're too good to lose but I am the best. Remember that, and I will tell you about my seafood recipes first."

The Nephew broke into a hearty laugh. He knew he had gotten to his dear old Uncle, and he was glad. It was a time in the Old Uncle's life that he wanted him to have some fire. Well, he does still have it.

"I'm listening, Old Uncle."

Now the Old Uncle had his time to laugh.

"Listen well, dear Nephew. You could learn something."

"Okay, Okay, shoot me down."

Somehow, neither man brought up the recipes again. It was all about riding together. It almost seemed that the two chefs had decided not to give in to the other. Yes, the rivalry had reached a boiling point. They loved each other, but the competition was real.

THE OLD UNCLE'S STUFFED SEASONED FLOUNDER FILLETS

INGREDIENTS & UTENSILS

Servings - 4

- ❐ 4 Fresh FLOUNDER FILLETS *(6-8 oz each)*
- ❐ 1 lb LUMP CRAB MEAT *(or claw meat)*
- ❐ 1 lb SHRIMP, cut in small pieces
- ❐ VEGETABLE SPRAY
- ❐ 1 Tbls CANOLA OIL
- ❐ CELERY, chopper fine
- ❐ 2 Tbls ONION, chopped fine
- ❐ 2 Tbls BELL PEPPER, cleaned and chopped
- ❐ 1 Tbls chopped FRESH BASIL
- ❐ 1 Tbls ANAHEIM CHILI PEPPER, cleaned, seeded, and chopped
- ❐ 1 cup JAPANESE BREAD CRUMBS *(Find these if possible. They are marvelous. If not, substitute Regular Bread Crumbs)*
- ❐ 1 Tbls MAYONNAISE (low fat)
- ❐ 1 teas LIME JUICE
- ❐ 1/2 teas RED PEPPER FLAKES
- ❐ 1 EGG WHITE, slightly beaten
- ❐ Touch of SALT
- ❐ 4 Tbls MELTED BUTTER
- ❐ 4 Tbls WHITE WINE
- ❐ 1 1/2 Tbls AMARETTO LIQUEUR
- ❐ ROSEMARY, BASIL, and BLACK PEPPER
- ❐ Small skillet to saute
- ❐ Small pot for boiling
- ❐ Cutting board and knife
- ❐ Sauce pan
- ❐ Large Casserole Dish
- ❐ Aluminum Foil

The Old Uncle's Stuffed Seasoned Flounder Fillets are continued on the next two pages!

THE OLD UNCLE'S STUFFED SEASONED FLOUNDER FILLETS

Continued

METHOD OF PREPARATION

First, boil the 1 lb of SHRIMP, and set aside.

In a medium saute pan, add:

- VEGETABLE SPRAY
- 1 Tbls CANOLA OIL

When warm, add:

- 2 Tbls CELERY, finely chopped
- 2 Tbls ONION, chopped fine
- 2 Tbls BELL PEPPER, cleaned and chopped fine
- 1 Tbls ANAHEIM CHILI PEPPER, cleaned, seeded, and chopped fine. *(Substitute Poblano or New Mexico)*

When onions are translucent, add:

- 1 cup JAPANESE BREAD CRUMBS
- 1 Tbls MAYONNAISE, low fat
- 1 teas LIME JUICE
- 1/2 teas RED PEPPER FLAKES
- 1 lb CRAB MEAT
- 1 lb Boiled SHRIMP, cut in small pieces

Now, mix it all together, and taste it. If it needs a little salt, add it, if not, let it go. Remember, you are the CHEF! Mix in the EGG WHITE. It won't make it stick together, but it will moisten it well.

Now, take the 4 FLOUNDER FILLETS, and make a cut long ways in the center of the fillet, being careful not to cut it all the way through. Now make another cut crosswise,

THE OLD UNCLE'S STUFFED SEASONED FLOUNDER FILLETS

Continued

right through the first cut. With a small knife, open up the cuts so you now have 4 flaps of fish in the center of the fillet.

With a medium spoon, stuff the fillets as equally as possible, using all the stuffing. If some stuffing is left, make a round ball of it, and cook it with the fish fillets.
Warm the 4 Tbls BUTTER, 4 Tbls WHITE WINE, and the 1 1/2 oz AMARETTO LIQUEUR together. When Butter is melted, brush the fillets with the mixture. Save what's left to do it again when they come out of the oven. Sprinkle the fillets with the ROSEMARY, BASIL, and BLACK PEPPER spices.

Place the stuffed fillets carefully into a large casserole dish, sprayed with Vegetable Spray.

Cover with ALUMINUM FOIL, and seal around the edges. Bake at 350 degrees for thirty minutes. Remove the foil and continue cooking until the fillets flake. It will probably take another 10 or 15 minutes.

Remove from the oven, and spoon the rest of the sauce over the fillets, mainly where the stuffing is.

It should make you proud!

THE OLD UNCLE'S SICILIANO FILLET OF SOLE

Servings - 4

Note - A tasty, yet easy dish

Ingredients & Utensils

- ❒ 4 - 6 oz FILLET OF SOLE *(or any other mild white fish)*
- ❒ VEGETABLE SPRAY
- ❒ 2 Tbls OLIVE OIL
- ❒ 20 oz Peeled and diced TOMATOES *(Fresh or Canned)*
- ❒ 2 Tbls FRESH BASIL, chopped or 2 teas Dried
- ❒ 2 Tbls BLACK OLIVES, pitted and chopped
- ❒ 2 Tbls GREEN OLIVES, pitted and chopped
- ❒ 2 Tbls FRESH CILANTRO, chopped
- ❒ 1 JALAPENO, seeded, cleaned and chopped
- ❒ SALT, BLACK PEPPER, and GARLIC POWDER to taste
- ❒ Medium skillet
- ❒ Large Casserole Dish
- ❒ Fork
- ❒ Chopping board and Knife

Method of Preparation

In a medium or large skillet, add VEGETABLE SPRAY and 2 Tbls OLIVE OIL.

When oil is warm, add 4 - 6 oz FILLET OF SOLE.

Lightly saute or fry for about 2 minutes on each side. Set aside.

THE OLD UNCLE'S SICILIANO FILLET OF SOLE

Continued

In a large casserole dish, place:

- 20 oz Peeled and diced TOMATOES *(Fresh or canned).*
- 2 Tbls FRESH BASIL, chopped
- 2 Tbls BLACK OLIVES, pitted and chopped
- 2 Tbls GREEN OLIVES, pitted and chopped
- 2 Tbls FRESH CILANTRO, chopped
- 1 JALAPENO, seeded, cleaned, chopped

When the above barely starts to boil, add previously fried Fillet of Sole pieces, carefully placing them on top of the tomato mixture so as not to burn yourself. Spoon sauce on top of them, and cook on 350 for 7-8 minutes.

When ready, season with a little SALT, BLACK PEPPER, and GARLIC POWDER.

A delicious easy recipe. Enjoy!

Pasquale Provenzano and wife, the Old Uncle's grandparents.

THE OLD UNCLE'S STUFFED CRABS ALLA JENNIE PRO

Servings - 4 This is my Mother's recipe for Stuffed Crabs. I consider her the finest cook across the board that I ever saw. Once she reached complete satisfaction on a dish, she never desired to make it again. She had accomplished her purpose - PERFECTION!.

INGREDIENTS & UTENSILS

- ❒ 1 1/4 lbs Fresh CRAB MEAT *(or 3 - 6 1/2 oz cans)*
- ❒ 1/2 cup CRACKER CRUMBS divided. *(I buy the salt free kind, and crush them with a rolling pin.)*
- ❒ VEGETABLE SPRAY
- ❒ 1 teas CANOLA OIL
- ❒ 1/4 cup CELERY, chopped fine
- ❒ 1 Tbls ONION, chopped fine
- ❒ 1 Tbls BELL PEPPER, chopped fine
- ❒ 1 Tbls LIME JUICE
- ❒ 1 Tbls MAYONNAISE, light or fat free
- ❒ 1/4 teas RED PEPPER FLAKES
- ❒ 1 EGG WHITE
- ❒ SALT
- ❒ 1 teas BUTTER on top of each individual crab shell or dish .
- ❒ Chopping board and knife
- ❒ Large bowl and mixing spoon
- ❒ Small saute skillet
- ❒ Measuring utensils
- ❒ Cleaned Crab Shells or small individual glasses or ceramic dishes

METHOD OF PREPARATION

Saute until soft *(using VEGETABLE SPRAY and 1 teas CANOLA OIL)*

- 1/4 cup CELERY chopped fine
- 1 Tbls ONION chopped fine
- 1 Tbls BELL PEPPER, chopped fine

Place 1 1/4 lbs Fresh CRAB MEAT in a large bowl. *(If you decided on the*

THE OLD UNCLE'S STUFFED CRABS ALLA JENNIE PRO

Continued

canned crab, be sure and wash it to remove most of the added salt.)

Now add:
- 1/4 cup CRACKER CRUMBS *(reserving the other 1/4 cup)*
- 1 Tbls LIME JUICE
- 1 Tbls MAYONNAISE
- 1/4 teas RED PEPPER FLAKES
- 1 EGG WHITE

Lightly sprinkle with a little SALT

Mix well, then add the sauteed ingredients above. Mix well again. The egg white will only moisten it a little but will not stick it together. Mix well, using your hands to do a thorough job.

Spray the crab shells or dishes with vegetable spray. Stuff them with the crab mixture. You should have enough to fill eight shells or small dishes. At two per person, this is just right.

Now place the other 1/4 cup of Cracker Crumbs into a flat small dish. Carefully, roll each shell or dish over the crumbs, and some will stick to it. When completed, put a teas of melted BUTTER on top of each crab.

We usually make these a day ahead of time, keeping them in the refrigerator, but if you prefer, you could do it all in one day.

Bake at 350 degrees for about 15 minutes. Fit for a King and a Queen !!!!

THE NEPHEW'S SHRIMP PARMESAN WITH PASTA

Servings - 2

INGREDIENTS AND UTENSILS

- ❒ 8 Extra Large SHRIMP butterflied *(Or 16 Medium)*

FOR DREDGING:

- ❒ FLOUR season with SALT and PEPPER
- ❒ 2 Medium EGGS slightly beaten
- ❒ ITALIAN BREAD CRUMBS sprinkled with PARMESAN CHEESE
- ❒ OLIVE OIL to saute or fry
- ❒ 6 oz PASTA of your choice
- ❒ 3 qts WATER slightly salted
- ❒ 12 oz MARINARA SAUCE *(Your choice, From the book or store bought)*
- ❒ 2 TBLS Grated PARMESAN CHEESE
- ❒ 1/2 cup Grated MOZZARELLA CHEESE
- ❒ 3 small bowls for dredging
- ❒ Large ovenproof skillet to saute or fry Shrimp *(may use deep-fryer)*
- ❒ Large pot to boil pasta
- ❒ Aluminum foil
- ❒ Two warmed small platters or dishes

METHOD OF PREPARATION

First, dredge the 8 Extra Large SHRIMP in the Flour, previously seasoned with salt and pepper.

Second, dredge the Shrimp in the slightly beaten Eggs.

Third, dredge the Shrimp in the Italian Seasoned Bread Crumbs, previously seasoned with Parmesan Cheese.

THE NEPHEW'S SHRIMP PARMESAN WITH PASTA

Continued

Place 3 qts slightly salted water on to boil the pasta.

Fry or saute shrimp in a large skillet until golden brown.

When the water boils, add the 6 oz pasta.

When the shrimp are done, drain the skillet. Add a little of the 12 oz MARINARA SAUCE to the bottom of the skillet. Place the shrimp in two circles *(one for each serving) with* the tails touching. Wrap the tails together with ALUMINUM FOIL, until bound together.

Pour part of the remaining Marinara Sauce over the Shrimp.
Sprinkle with:
- 2 Tbls PARMESAN CHEESE
- 1/2 cup Grated MOZZARELLA CHEESE

Place in the broiler. *(Watch closely!)* Remove when cheese begins to turn a little brown.

Pour the remainder of the Marinara Sauce over the now cooked Pasta. Place half the pasta on the side of the warmed platters or dishes. Then slide the shrimp, cheese and pasta on to the other side.

Enjoy. Remember, you're the chef now!

THE OLD UNCLE'S CLASSIC SMOKED SALMON

Servings - 2 or 3 If you are cooking just to eat dinner or supper, leave this one alone. If PRIDE enters into your cooking, then baby, this one's for you. - The Old Uncle

If using a water smoker, place a choice of the following in the water— beer, any old liqueur, fruit juice, cider, wine or whatever. I use a small metal electric smoker that heats the wood on the bottom, and the low temperature makes it ideal. Use low heat and lots of smoke.

INGREDIENTS & UTENSILS

- ❒ 1 lb SALMON FILLETS or STEAKS
- ❒ 1 qt WATER
- ❒ 1/3 cup BROWN SUGAR packed
- ❒ 3 TBLS SALT
- ❒ Good Sprinkling of BLACK PEPPER
- ❒ Light sprinkling of RED PEPPER FLAKES
- ❒ 4 oz BEER *(preferably not light beer)*
- ❒ 1/4 cup BROWN SUGAR
- ❒ 1/2 teas GARLIC POWDER
- ❒ 1/2 teas DRIED OREGANO
- ❒ 1/2 teas DRIED BASIL
- ❒ 1 1/2 - 2 qt Glass or ceramic dish to marinate
- ❒ 1 1/2 - 2 qt Aluminum Pan for smoking
- ❒ Supplies for your smoker or barbecue grill
- ❒ Charcoal
- ❒ Hardwood pieces or chips

METHOD OF PREPARATION

Place in a 1 1/2 or 2 qt Glass or Ceramic Dish:

- 1 lb of SALMON FILLETS or STEAKS.
- Add 1 qt of WATER

Sprinkle with:

- 1/3 cup of BROWN SUGAR
- 3 TBLS SALT

Now, sprinkle with BLACK PEPPER and lightly sprinkle with RED PEPPER FLAKES

The next day, to smoke, use either method:

1. THE WATER SMOKER

Light the Charcoal in the bottom pan. When it is ready *(gray with no flames)* Add the soaked hardwood chips or pieces.

THE OLD UNCLE'S CLASSIC SMOKED SALMON

Now, place the water pan in place. Add whatever liquid you choose to use. It could be just water, or you can use many of the choices listed under Ingredients & Utensils.

Now, add the top rack. During the cooking process, you can add additional wood pieces or chips through the little door at the bottom.

2. Barbecue Grill

Put the charcoal on the bottom of the grill on one side. On the other side, place a water pan, filled with a liquid. It could be water or whatever. Light the charcoal, and when its ready, gray with no flames, add the soaked hardwood chips on the fire.

You can add more soaked chips or water while cooking. Be sure and place the salmon directly over the water pan, and use low heat. *(not too much charcoal)*

To Prepare the Salmon

The next day, remove the marinade dish from the refrigerator.

Remove the Salmon and discard the marinade.

Now, rinse the salmon lightly, and pat dry with paper towels.

The Old Uncle's Classic Smoked Salmon is continued on the next page!

THE OLD UNCLE'S CLASSIC SMOKED SALMON

Continued

Let it air out for about a half hour or so. Now spray an Aluminum Foil Pan *(available at all grocery stores)* with Vegetable Spray, and place the Salmon in the pan. Pour about 4 oz Beer over the Salmon.

Now, Sprinkle with:
- 1/4 cup Brown Sugar
- 1/2 teas Garlic Powder
- 1/2 teas Oregano
- 1/2 teas Basil

Now, with a teaspoon, dip up the beer and drizzle over the fillets, saturating them with the spices and beer.

Place the Salmon on the ready grill. Leave it alone and let it do it's thing. It's impossible for me to tell you how long it will take. Probably at least three hours, but it could take as long as 5.

If it needs more beer, add a touch. However this recipe is different than almost all other recipes. It will be difficult to overcook it. If it gets too much juice in the pan, after three hours, pour most of it out.

I usually cook extra. It freezes great. Thaw it out, and pour a little beer, and add the spices. Delicious.

In fact, if it cools off before you are ready to eat, add a little beer and spices, and warm it in the oven.

Good luck and good eating.

THE NEPHEW'S SNAPPER D'AMICO

A featured Dish in the D'Amico Italian Market Cafe

Servings -2

Serving Suggestion - Use 1/4 wedge of lemon and one sprig of parsley for each dish. Serve with a side dish of Linguini Pasta covered with Marinara Sauce. ENJOY!

INGREDIENTS & UTENSILS

- ❒ 2 - 8 oz SNAPPER FILLETS
- ❒ Small dish of FLOUR for dredging
- ❒ 2 - slightly beaten EGGS for dredging
- ❒ 2 - oz Virgin Olive Oil
- ❒ 2 - teas PINE NUTS
- ❒ 1/4 teas Minced GARLIC
- ❒ 4 oz WHITE WINE
- ❒ 3 oz BUTTER
- ❒ 1/2 oz LEMON JUICE
- ❒ 4 oz LUMP CRAB MEAT
- ❒ 2 small dishes for dredging
- ❒ 1 medium saute pan
- ❒ 1 medium oven pan

Snapper D'Amico

The Nephew's Snapper D'Amico is continued on the next page!

THE NEPHEW'S SNAPPER D'AMICO

Continued

METHOD OF PREPARATION

Salt and Pepper 2 - 8 oz SNAPPER FILLETS Arrange 2 small dishes for dredging - one with FLOUR and one with 2 slightly beaten EGGS.

In a medium saute pan, place 2 oz VIRGIN OLIVE OIL and warm. Add the 2 - 8 oz SNAPPER FILLETS and saute until golden brown on both sides. To assure the fish is really cooked, put the fillets in a pan and place in the oven at 350 degrees for a few minutes.

Discard juice in saute pan, and add 2 teas PINE NUTS. Toast them first, then add the 1/4 teas Minced GARLIC and saute briefly.

Now add 4 oz WHITE WINE and cook until reduced by 50 Percent. Then add 3 oz BUTTER and 1/2 oz LEMON JUICE and cook for about a minute

Finally, at the last minute, toss in the 4 oz LUMP CRAB MEAT. Stir and remove from the fire. Now the sauce is ready to add over the fish fillets. You will be proud of this one.

THE NEPHEW'S SNAPPER ALLA CAPELLINI

Servings - 2 This recipe will make you a genuine CHEF. Imagine! Rolling Pasta around the fish. You can do it!

Serving suggestion: Garnish with 1/4 lemon wedge and a parsley sprig. A good side dish would be pasta topped with Marinara Sauce.

INGREDIENTS & UTENSILS

- ❒ 2 - 8 oz SNAPPER FILLETS, seasoned with Salt and Pepper
- ❒ 2 small dishes, one for FLOUR, and one for 2 lightly beaten eggs for dredging.
- ❒ 6 oz Cooked Capellini Pasta, with a little extra Olive Oil added.
- ❒ 2 oz VIRGIN OLIVE OIL
- ❒ 2 teas Melted BUTTER
- ❒ 1 oz LEMON JUICE
- ❒ 1 teas CAPERS
- ❒ 4 Diced Roma TOMATOES
- ❒ 4 oz WHITE WINE
- ❒ 2 teas WHIPPING CREAM
- ❒ 4 Sauteed JUMBO SHRIMP

METHOD OF PREPARATION

Boil 6 oz CAPELLINI PASTA with a little extra Olive Oil added.

Salt and Pepper the 2 - 8 oz SNAPPER FILLETS. In 2 small dishes, place enough FLOUR in one for dredging and 2 slightly beaten EGGS in the other one.

Now comes the tricky part. Lay half the cooked pasta out on a board, lengthening it out as well as possible without spending too much time. Now lay a fillet crosswise and carefully wrap the fish in the cooked pasta. Repeat this with the other fillet and the other half of the pasta.

Place 2 oz OLIVE OIL in a medium saute

The Nephew's Snapper Alla Capellini is continued on the next page!

THE NEPHEW'S SNAPPER ALLA CAPELLINI

Continued

pan. Warm and then carefully add the wrapped fish fillets. Saute on both sides until golden brown.

Now remove the fish from the saute pan. Place it in an ovenproof pan and cook at 350 degrees for a couple of minutes to assure complete doneness.

Discard juice from the saute pan. Add 2 teas BUTTER, 1 oz LEMON JUICE, 1 teas CAPERS, 4 oz Diced Roma Tomatoes, and 4 oz WHITE WINE. Saute this sauce for about a minute. Then add 2 teas WHIPPING CREAM and saute another minute. Add 2 seasoned sauteed JUMBO SHRIMP to top each fillet. Now the sauce is ready to pour over the Fish and the Shrimp.

Snapper alla Capellini

PART FIVE:
VEGETABLES

From the wonderful soil of Italy

The Nephew and the Old Uncle sat in the back of the restaurant, both tired and needing to rest.

"Old Uncle, It's late and I'm tired. You're just plain old and lazy. Why don't we have a glass of wine. It might help us both."

"Oh, I'm old, no doubt about that, but that other part of your statement. You can it, cause it's not true and you know it."

The Nephew broke out in laughter. "I just love to get your dander up. Hell, I know you're anything but lazy, Old Man."

"If we're going to drink some wine, serve me the good stuff. You know, the kind you drink when you're alone."

"Old Uncle, you're just being ugly now. Taste this and tell me the truth."

The uncle sipped on it, and smiled. "It's good stuff, Nephew."

The Nephew smiled . "What you got on the docket for the new book on Vegetables?"

"I plan to use three of the recipes from our other book. The Eggplant Parmesan, the Stuffed Artichokes, and the Asparagus one. What do you have, Nephew?"

"Not so fast, dear Uncle. How about the new ones?"

" Oh, that slipped my mind. I got two new ones. One zinger with Spinach and Eggs, and another that features Mushrooms."

"Sounds great. I got an easy one with Cauliflower and Broccoli, and another that's going to be a natural, titled Stuffed Rolled Eggplants."

"That's a killer diller of a recipe. You know, these people who buy our book are going to be lucky."

"I hope you're right." laughed the Nephew.

THE NEPHEWS BROCCOLI AND CAULIFLOWER CASSEROLE

Servings - 6 - 8

Note - An easy but very tasty vegetable dish

Ingredients & Utensils

- ❒ 1 Head CAULIFLOWER
- ❒ 1 Head BROCCOLI
- ❒ 1 cup SEASONED WHITE BREAD CRUMBS
- ❒ 3/4 cup Grated ROMANO CHEESE
- ❒ 3 oz VIRGIN OLIVE OIL
- ❒ Measuring utensils
- ❒ Large Bowl
- ❒ 9 1/2 x 13 inch Casserole Dish.

Method of Preparation

In a large Bowl place:

- ◆ 1 head CAULIFLOWER, chopped
- ◆ 1 head BROCCOLI, cut into small pieces
- ◆ 1 cup Seasoned WHITE BREAD CRUMBS
- ◆ 3/4 cup Grated ROMANO CHEESE
- ◆ 3 oz VIRGIN OLIVE OIL

Mix together until sticky. Evenly distribute all of the ingredients. Bake uncovered in a 350 degree oven for 20 minutes.

The Nephews Mom & Dad, on the couch at Maw Maw Jennie's house on Polk St.

THE OLD UNCLE'S SPINACH AND EGGS

INGREDIENTS & UTENSILS

Servings - 4

- ❒ 5 - large EGGS hard boiled
- ❒ 2 - 9 oz Pkg. Frozen SPINACH
- ❒ 1 cup Grated ROMANO CHEESE divided
- ❒ 2/3 cup HALF and HALF divided
- ❒ 2/3 cup Seasoned BREAD CRUMBS divided
- ❒ SALT and PEPPER to taste
- ❒ Cutting board and knife
- ❒ 9 inch ovenproof dish

METHOD OF PREPARATION

Boil 5 large EGGS. When cool, slice them and set aside.

Prepare 2 Pkg of Frozen SPINACH as to instructions on the box. When cool, chop SPINACH and place one carton in the bottom of a 9 inch ovenproof dish.

Pour 1/2 of the HALF and HALF over the spinach. Sprinkle with half of the Cup of Grated ROMANO CHEESE.

Sprinkle with half of the cup of Seasoned BREAD CRUMBS.

Space half of the sliced 5 EGGS on the Spinach. Season with Salt and Pepper. Now repeat this for the next layer.

Bake at 350 degrees for 25 minutes.

THE NEPHEW'S ROLLED STUFFED EGGPLANT

Servings - 2

Note - A Recipe that you will enjoy making and more than that - eating it!

Ingredients & Utensils

- ❒ 2 oz OLIVE OIL
- ❒ 12 - slices EGGPLANT, 1/8" slice with skin
- ❒ 8 oz CHEESE RAVIOLI STUFFING *(q.v.)*
- ❒ 12 oz of The Nephew's Marinara Sauce
- ❒ 5 oz LINGUINI Pasta
- ❒ 2 pinches Grated ROMANO CHEESE
- ❒ 4 oz SEASONED BREAD CRUMBS
- ❒ Sharp knife
- ❒ Large Saute Pan
- ❒ 1 or 2 large ovenproof baking plates
- ❒ 2 small platters for serving

Method of Preparation

In 2 oz OLIVE OIL, lightly saute 12 slices of EGGPLANTS, 1/8" thick.

Meanwhile boil 5 oz of LINGUINI PASTA

Remove Eggplants slices from saute pan and dry with paper towels. Now coat both sides with Seasoned BREAD CRUMBS. Using 3/4 oz of Cheese Ravioli Stuffing on each slice of Eggplant, and roll each one into a cylinder.

Put a small amount of MARINARA SAUCE on 2 ovenproof plates. Now put half of the Rolled Eggplants on each plate. Cover each Eggplant dish with Marinara Sauce.

Toss cooked LINGUINI with remaining Marinara Sauce.

Serve 6 Rolled Stuffed Eggplant and Linguini Pasta topped with Marinara Sauce on each platter.

Garnish with a pinch of Grated ROMANO CHEESE and PARSLEY Sprigs.

THE OLD UNCLE'S ASPARAGUS WITH PARMESAN

INGREDIENTS & UTENSILS

Servings - 2 - 3

❐ 1 lb Fresh ASPARAGUS
❐ 2 Tbls Melted BUTTER
❐ 2 Tbls Grated PARMESAN CHEESE
(More if you like it like. We do!)
❐ Sharp knife
❐ Steamer or pot for boiling
❐ Baking dish that accommodates asparagus in a single layer.

METHOD OF PREPARATION

Thoroughly wash 1lb of Fresh ASPARAGUS

Cut off all the tough part on the bottoms.

Scrape off the scales, cutting off all the outer skin.

Wash again.

Steam until tender *(or boil)*

Line up asparagus, single file, in a baking dish.

Drizzle 2Tbls Melted BUTTER over asparagus.

Sprinkle 2Tbls or more of grated PARMESAN CHEESE

Place in a broiler uncovered. and watch closely. When the cheese begins to change color, it is ready. If no broiler is available, use the oven at 475 degrees.

THE OLD UNCLE'S STUFFED ARTICHOKES

Servings - 4 — Based on 1/2 artichoke per person

INGREDIENTS & UTENSILS

- ❒ 2 Fresh ARTICHOKES *(medium to large)*
- ❒ 2 cups Seasoned BREAD CRUMBS
- ❒ 2 Tbls OLIVE OIL
- ❒ 2 Tbls WATER
- ❒ Cutting board, knife, and scissors
- ❒ Teaspoon to fill artichoke leaves
- ❒ Pan or casserole dish with a cover

METHOD OF PREPARATION

Cut off the stem on the bottom and about a 1/2 inch from the top of 2 medium to large ARTICHOKES. The removal of the stem will enable the artichokes to stand on their own. Using scissors, nip the points off all the leaves. Grab the artichoke by the bottom, and beat it, top down, several times on the cutting board, forcing the leaves to open. Finally, use your fingers to help.

Wash the artichokes in cool water, and let them drain for a few minutes.

Meanwhile, measure out 1 cup of Seasoned Bread Crumbs for each artichoke.

Using a teaspoon, fill in all the leaves with the bread crumbs, starting at the bottom and circling around it. Again, use your fingers to help open the leaves. Repeat the method with the other artichoke. Filled properly, it should take the full cup of crumbs for each one.

THE OLD UNCLE'S STUFFED ARTICHOKES

Continued

Now, on each artichoke, drizzle:

- One Tbls OLIVE OIL
- One Tbls WATER

Place in a dish or casserole dish with a cover. Add about a 1/2 inch of water. Bake covered at 350 degrees for one hour.

However, after 30 minutes, check the water level. Bring level back to the original 1/2 inch.

After one full hour, check for doneness. Pull out a couple of leaves. If they come out easy, they're ready. If not, cook a little more.

Artichokes freeze well, so you might want to do more than 2 at a time. If so, when fully cooked and cool, wrap each one in foil, and slide into a plastic bag.

Enjoy. It's an Italian delicacy

The Old Uncle's brother, Foley and his lovely wife, Pat.

THE OLD UNCLE'S EGGPLANT PARMESAN

Servings — 2

Note — Used as an Entree dish in most Italian Restaurants, this is positively a class dish.

INGREDIENTS & UTENSILS

- ❐ 1 Large EGGPLANT peeled and cut into 1/4" to 1/2" slices
- ❐ 1 Tbls SALT
- ❐ VEGETABLE SPRAY
- ❐ 16 oz can PEELED WHOLE TOMATOES
- ❐ 6 oz can TOMATO PASTE
- ❐ 6 oz can WATER *(using same can that held tomato paste)*
- ❐ 2 teas DRIED OREGANO or 2 Tbls Fresh
- ❐ 2 teas DRIED BASIL or 2 Tbls Fresh
- ❐ 2 teas GARLIC POWDER
- ❐ SALT and PEPPER for sprinkling
- ❐ ITALIAN SEASONED BREAD CRUMBS
- ❐ Grated PARMESAN CHEESE
- ❐ 2 oz MOZZARELLA CHEESE
- ❐ 1 Tbls OLIVE OIL
- ❐ Pan for soaking eggplant
- ❐ Colander
- ❐ Medium pan or casserole dish
- ❐ Cookie Sheet
- ❐ 9" Casserole dish or something similar

METHOD OF PREPARATION

Peel 1 large EGGPLANT and slice it into 1/4 to 1/2 inch slices. Soak in water and 1 Tbls SALT for approximately 10 minutes. Rinse in warm water and drain in a colander. Pat dry with paper towels.

Spray a cookie sheet with VEGETABLE SPRAY. Place Eggplant slices on the sheet. Spray again, and sprinkle with Salt and Pepper. Bake at 375 degrees until lightly

THE OLD UNCLE'S EGGPLANT PARMESAN

Continued

browned. *(about 5 minutes)* Turn and continue baking until equally browned.

Now, make the sauce. In a medium pan or dish, place:

- 1 - 16 oz can Peeled Whole TOMATOES, chopped keeping all the juice
- 1 - 6 oz can TOMATO PASTE
- 1 - 6 oz can WATER *(using same tomato paste can)*
- 1 Tbls OLIVE OIL
- 2 teas DRIED OREGANO
- 2 teas DRIED BASIL
- 2 teas GARLIC POWDER
- Sprinkle of SALT and PEPPER

Cook on low heat for 30 Minutes. Spray a 9 inch Casserole or similar dish with Vegetable Spray. Barely cover the bottom with some of the sauce. Place browned Eggplant pieces in a single layer, making it fit by cutting pieces if necessary. Sprinkle with Italian seasoned BREAD CRUMBS, and GRATED PARMESAN CHEESE.

Starting with the sauce again, repeat above applications. Then follow with the sauce again, the Parmesan Cheese, and finally, add 2 oz Grated MOZZARELLA CHEESE on top.

Bake at 350 degrees for 20 Minutes. If sauce is allowed to cool before putting the Parmesan together, then you will have to cook it longer

THE OLD UNCLE'S STUFFED PEPPERS

Servings — 3 - 4

INGREDIENTS AND UTENSILS

- ❐ 4 Large or 6 medium BELL PEPPERS, green, red, or yellow *(I prefer Red ones)*
- ❐ Slightly Salted WATER
- ❐ 2 Tbls OIL
- ❐ 1 lb Ground BEEF
- ❐ 3 Tbls chopped ONION
- ❐ 2 Tbls chopped GARLIC
- ❐ 1 rib CELERY, chopped fine
- ❐ 2 Tbls DRIED PARSLEY
- ❐ 2 Tbls BLACK PEPPER
- ❐ 2 teas SALT
- ❐ 1/2 cup diced MUSHROOMS
- ❐ Grated ROMANO CHEESE
- ❐ Pot large enough to boil bell peppers
- ❐ Knife and chopping board
- ❐ Large Skillet
- ❐ Saute Pan for Mushrooms

METHOD OF PREPARATION

Boil 4 Large or 6 Small BELL PEPPERS *(Red, Green or Yellow)* in a large pot with slightly salted water to cover. After boiling 5 minutes, remove from fire, and take peppers out to let dry. Set aside.

In a large Skillet with 2 Tbls OIL, place:

- 1 lb Ground BEEF
- 3 Tbls chopped ONIONS
- 2 Tbls chopped GARLIC CLOVES
- 1 rib CELERY, chopped fine
- 2 Tbls DRIED PARSLEY
- 2 Tbls BLACK PEPPER
- 2 teas SALT

THE OLD UNCLE'S STUFFED PEPPERS

Continued

Brown until Ground BEEF is no longer pink.

Now, saute 1/2 cup diced MUSHROOMS

Combine the Ground Beef Mixture with the Mushrooms, and mix well.

Stuff the BELL PEPPERS with the mixture. If there is extra stuffing, place it around the Peppers in the roasting pan.

Sprinkle with Grated ROMANO CHEESE, and Bake at 350 degrees for about 25 minutes.

ENJOY!

The Nephew's father, Nash Sr. with his twin brother, Sam and their sister Esther Mae (the Old Uncle's wife) at their first Holy Communion.

PART SIX:

ANTIPASTO!

The fun dish of Old Italy

The Old Uncle and the Nephew sat out in the patio area of the D'AMICO ITALIAN MARKET CAFE. It was a good location to observe the customers coming in and out of the restaurant.

"Nephew, have you noticed the ages of most of the customers? It seems the younger generation has a real taste for good Italian food."

"Yes, Old Uncle. Many of the younger people are moving toward the classical style cooking."

The Old Uncle nodded, "Very interesting, Nephew. I believe we should stick to the same type of antipasto as before."

"I definitely agree. However, maybe one major change. Why don't we just handle it together?"

"Excellent thinking, dear Nephew. But you know, maybe we are carrying this a little far. We never seem to get along. You think it might hurt our reputation?"

"Let's keep it our secret. It'll probably be fun not to battle with you for a while."

"Righto," laughed the Old Uncle. "For a while. Let's don't over do this."

"Agreed" said the Nephew as he giggled a little.

Antipasto!

ANTIPASTO !

The classic Italian before-dinner dish that combines the American salad and appetizer dishes.

Depending on who the guests will be, and how far you might want to go, we are offering 2 types of Antipasto Trays.

First, the Regular Antipasto, where everything listed can be purchased in a food establishment of some type.

Listed below are 25 varieties for your Antipasto Tray. However, we suggest, for the average Dinner Party, *(4 to 8 Guests),* a selection of 10 varieties from the list. If it is a larger party, you probably should increase the number of items.

We suggest using at least two items from each of the four types listed.

MEATS

Mortadella
(Italian Bologna)
Genoa Salami
Prosciutto
(Italian Ham)

FISH

Anchovies
Sardines
Tuna
Salmon
Crab

VEGETABLES

Artichoke Hearts
Mushrooms
Green Olives
Black Olives
Tomatoes
Caponata
Red Bell Peppers
Radishes
Pimiento
Chili Peppers

CHEESES

Mozzarella
Parmesan
Ricotta
Romano
Provolone
Caciocavallo

ANTIPASTO

MEATS

All three of the meats should be sliced very thin. Roll each thin piece and stick a toothpick through it for an individual serving. Prosciutto is excellent when attached to a small bite size piece of melon, cantaloupe or sweetened pears or apples. American bologna, salami, or ham can be substituted but slice it thin. If possible, serve the Italian meats.

FISH

While the Sardines are served as is, and the canned. Tuna and Salmon may be served in chunks or smaller pieces, the Anchovy may be served wrapped around a caper, and held together with a toothpick. Crab meat can be served on a small cracker or thin toast.

VEGETABLES

Delicious Artichoke Hearts can be bought in jars or cans. If you choose Black Olives, buy the Italian ones - ripe and seedless. Use fresh, ripe, sliced Pimentos should be served plain. The Red Pimiento will add a lot of color to your Tray. Green Bell Peppers can be served fresh or marinated in Italian Dressing. A very special item will be the Caponata. An eggplant dish that is sold in cans that are almost as delicious as anyone can make at home.

Now, to the recipes that follow. The small whole Mushrooms are delicious and easy to prepare. The Green Olives are a sentimental favorite of the Old Uncle. It is his Mother's recipe, and he still has it in her handwriting. Crushed Green Olives could never be better.

CHEESES

All except the soft Ricotta can be served in small thin slices. Soft Ricotta is served with a spoon or on a small cracker. However, there is a Dry Ricotta that is delicious, and it can be served in small pieces. Caciocavallo is expensive, and many times, hard to find. If you find some, buy it. Give yourself a treat.

Now to the Deluxe Antipasto Tray. It is a tray made from many special items, and while it is more work, for the right party, it could be worth it. However, before we scare you off it, the meats and cheese would be practically the same, using only the imported ones. A third choice would be, and it would be a
good one, make a couple of the recipes listed (all are easy), and use only imported meats and cheeses.

- ❒ Grilled Eggplant Slices *(recipe follows)*
- ❒ Fried Zucchini *(recipe follows)*
- ❒ Roasted Red Bell Peppers *(recipe follows)*
- ❒ Marinated Vegetables *(Cracked Green Olives and Marinated Mushrooms follow)*
- ❒ Risotto Balls *(make this one, don't leave it out. Recipe follows)*

THE DELUXE ANTIPASTO ALLA ITALIANO TRAY

GRILLED OR SAUTEED EGGPLANT

1/4 inch slices of EGGPLANTS. *(We suggest the Japanese variety, where you can make small round slices easily because of the shape. Use Olive Oil, and season with salt and pepper.)*

FRIED ZUCCHINI

Fry Zucchini slices in deep Olive Oil. Always season when removing anything from being fried.

ROASTED RED BELL PEPPERS

Cover Peppers with water and boil for about 5 minutes. Remove from fire, and place in a paper bag, checking after 10 minutes to see if skin peels off easily. If not, put them back in the bag and close it again for a few more minutes. When skin is removed, remove the stems, seeds, cleaning the inside good. Now cut them into strips and they are ready. Delicious.

MARINATED WHOLE MUSHROOMS

Select pretty whole fresh MUSHROOMS and saute in a skillet with BUTTER. When cool, place in a jar and cover with ITALIAN SALAD DRESSING. Put the top on the jar, and place in the refrigerator overnight.

You can use many other Italian vegetables the same way.

THE DELUXE ANTIPASTO ALLA ITALIANO TRAY

CRUSHED ITALIAN GREEN OLIVES

INGREDIENTS AND UTENSILS

- ❒ 1 lb ITALIAN GREEN OLIVES
- ❒ 1 cup CELERY, chopped in 1 inch pieces
- ❒ 2 cup chopped POBLANO CHILI PEPPERS
- ❒ 2 teas CAPERS
- ❒ 1 1/2 cups water
- ❒ 3/4 cup VINEGAR
- ❒ 1/3 cup OLIVE OIL
- ❒ 1 1/2 teas SALT
- ❒ 1/2 teas BLACK PEPPER
- ❒ Small hammer or bottle
- ❒ 1 qt Jar

METHOD OF PREPARATION

Hit each individual Olive with the hammer, being sure they mash a little. Place them in a quart jar. Add all above ingredients. Cover the jar, shake well, and place in the refrigerator.

Antipasto alla Italiano

THE DELUXE ANTIPASTO ALLA ITALIANO TRAY

RISOTTO BALLS

Ingredients and Utensils

- ❒ 1/2 oz Minced Peeled GARLIC
- ❒ 1 cup Finely Chopped YELLOW ONIONS
- ❒ 2 cups small diced ROMA TOMATOES
- ❒ 2 1/2 cups Seasoned WHITE BREAD CRUMBS
- ❒ 3/4 cup CHABLIS WINE
- ❒ 1/2 cup cleaned CRAB CLAW MEAT
- ❒ 5 beaten EGGS
- ❒ 1/2 cup all purpose FLOUR
- ❒ 1/2 cup BASIL LEAVES
- ❒ 6 cups cooked Aborio RICE
- ❒ Cutting board and knife
- ❒ Measuring Cup
- ❒ Wire Whip
- ❒ Tongs
- ❒ Mixing Bowl
- ❒ Stock Pot

Method of Preparation

In a large stock pot combine:

- 1/2 oz Minced Peeled GARLIC
- 1 cup finely chopped Yellow ONION
- 2 cups small diced ROMA TOMATOES
- 3/4 cup CHABLIS WINE

Put on low heat, and cook until reduced about one third.

Add 1 1/2 cups of Seasoned White BREAD CRUMBS and mix well in the pot. Remove from the heat and let it cool.

THE DELUXE ANTIPASTO ALLA ITALIANO TRAY

RISOTTO BALLS
continued

Add :
- 6 cups Cooked RICE
- 1/2 cup cleaned CRAB CLAW MEAT

Mix well.

Prepare for dredging with:
- Bowl of FLOUR
- Bowl of beaten EGGS
- Bowl of Seasoned White Bread Crumbs

Using your hands, roll mixture into 1 1/2 oz Balls. Set aside. Now, once all mixture has been rolled, begin the dredging process.

Roll each ball thoroughly in the flour dish, followed by the egg mixture, and finally in the seasoned bread crumbs.

When all have been battered, deep fry in hot oil until all are golden brown.

Time consuming? Yes. But well worth the effort and time. They are truly good.

If you have a LAZY SUSAN, it is perfect for your Antipasto creation. It is a revolving deal that enables the guests to easily get the next item they want to try. If not, a large platter or board of some type will have to suffice. Place curly lettuce leaves all over the bottom of whatever you decide to use. While some of your selections will require dishes, some can be placed right on the lettuce. The more crowded the tray looks, the more appealing it will be to the guests. Try to arrange the colors so as to make it even more appealing.

Regardless of what else you serve that evening, I can assure you the Antipasto Tray will be on their minds for a long time. Make a big splash. Try it and see how successful it can be!

PART SEVEN: SOUPS

The stomach warming liquids of Old ITALY

The Nephew and the Old Uncle entered the crowded restaurant with a smile on their faces. It was a cold and mean day for people to be out.

The Nephew was proud of his establishment, D'AMICO ITALIAN MARKET CAFE. His loyal partner, Luke, was also all smiles, as they sat at the counter, with all the tables being occupied. Partnership is a delicate thing, but this time, it was a huge success.

The Old Uncle broke the silence. "Take a look around. Soup is really a big item when the weather's like this."

"Old man, you can be pretty smart at times. I see a lot of soup dishes."

"Our Tomato-Basil Soup is a good one, but I'll bet Minestrone runs out first. What you got in the book, Old Uncle?"

"I couldn't find anything better than Mamo Jennie's Chicken Soup. I stuck with it all the way."

"We will probably have another one, but I haven't decided on anything yet."

The Old Uncle laughed. "You don't have to keep it a secret. I won't steal it. Hell, I'll just ask your partner. He's honest."

"You old reprobate. You couldn't steal a nickel if someone put it in your greedy hands."

The Old Uncle smiled and kept quiet. To himself he thought: What a great Nephew. I love him like a son but that sharp devil will never know it. He grinned as he thought about the soups. Hell, My Nephew is no dummy. One look around, and you can see that the soup not mentioned is all over this place. New England Clam Chowder."

THE OLD UNCLE'S MAMO JENNIE'S CHICKEN SOUP

INGREDIENTS AND UTENSILS

Servings - 8

- ❒ 1 - 4 lb CHICKEN cut in pieces
- ❒ 20 GREEN ONIONS cut in 2" pieces, using both the green and white parts.
- ❒ 10 CARROTS, cut in 2 inch pieces
- ❒ 10 ribs CELERY, cut in 2 inch pieces
- ❒ 2 medium size TOMATOES, quartered
- ❒ 4 sprigs PARSLEY, roughly chopped
- ❒ 1 teas DRIED BASIL or 1 Tbls Fresh
- ❒ 2 teas SALT
- ❒ 2 teas BLACK PEPPER
- ❒ 3 qts HOT WATER
- ❒ 2 oz very small PASTA or very thin SPAGHETTI per Person *(Optional but very desirable)*
- ❒ Knife and cutting boards *(Always use different cutting boards for meats and vegetables.)*
- ❒ 6 qt Pot with cover
- ❒ Large spoon
- ❒ Medium pot to cook past

If you are going to freeze part of this soup, cook above amount per person, and add to the part of the soup you plan to eat. Of course, if you plan to use all the soup now, cook 16 oz pasta or spaghetti, in water, strain, and add to the completed soup. SALT, PEPPER, and grated PARMESAN or ROMANO CHEESE. Soup tastes vary, and letting each person season their own works very well.

The Old Uncle's beautiful Mother, Mamo Jennie.

THE OLD UNCLE'S MAMO JENNIE'S CHICKEN SOUP

Continued

Method of Preparation

Cut up a 4 lb CHICKEN, and place the pieces in a large pot that has been sprayed with vegetable spray.

Add -

- 20 - 2 inch pieces GREEN ONIONS
- 10 - 2 inch pieces CARROTS
- 10 - 2 inch pieces CELERY
- 2 medium size TOMATOES, quartered
- 4 sprigs Fresh PARSLEY, chopped
- 1 teas DRIED BASIL or 1 Tbls Fresh
- 2 teas SALT
- 2 teas BLACK PEPPER
- 3 quarts HOT WATER

Cover, bring to a boil, and simmer 2 - 2 1/2 hours until Chicken is very tender.

Remove the Chicken from the pot. Let it cool, and remove the meat from the bones, and take off any remaining skin.

Meanwhile, strain the soup, discarding all the vegetables. Place broth back in the pot, and after cooling some, skim off any fat.

Place chicken, now broken into small pieces, back in the broth. Cook on low heat for about 30 more minutes.

Cook in the other pot, 2 oz of small pasta or very thin spaghetti per person. If you plan to use all the soup now, use 16 oz of the pasta or spaghetti. Add a touch of salt and olive oil to the pot.

If saving some, divide the soup, and add the cooked pasta to the soup you plan to use now. Freeze the balance, remembering to add the pasta later. Serve with SALT, BLACK PEPPER, and ROMANO or PARMESAN CHEESE

THE NEPHEW'S MINESTRONE SOUP

Servings - 16

INGREDIENTS AND UTENSILS

- ❒ 3 Pts WATER
- ❒ 1 Pt CHICKEN STOCK
- ❒ 1/2 thinly sliced yellow ONION
- ❒ 1 1/2 ribs CELERY, diced
- ❒ 1 CARROT, diced
- ❒ 1 sliced ZUCCHINI
- ❒ 1 1/2 peeled and diced POTATOES
- ❒ 18 oz crushed TOMATOES
- ❒ 1 pinch Salt
- ❒ 1 pinch BLACK PEPPER
- ❒ 10 oz canned CANNELLINI BEANS

METHOD OF PREPARATION

In a large pot, bring 3 Pts WATER and 1 Pt CHICKEN STOCK to a boil. Add 1 diced CARROT and 1 1/2 Russet POTATOES peeled and diced. Cook for 3 -5 minutes.

Now add :

- 1/2 thinly sliced Yellow Onions,
- 1 1/2 ribs CELERY, diced,
- 1 sliced ZUCCHINI,
- 18 oz crushed TOMATOES.

Bring to a boil again. Now add the pinch of SALT and BLACK PEPPER.

At the last minute, add the CANNELLINI BEANS. Let simmer and serve.

THE NEPHEW'S TOMATO AND BASIL SOUP

Servings - 5

Ingredients and Utensils

- ❒ 1 1/4 qts WHIPPING CREAM
- ❒ 1/8 teas minced peeled GARLIC
- ❒ 1/2 cup Grated ROMANO CHEESE
- ❒ 6 oz TOMATO SAUCE
- ❒ 1/8 cup chopped fresh BASIL LEAVES
- ❒ 1/2 Tbls BUTTER
- ❒ 1 oz CHICKEN STOCK
- ❒ SALT and BLACK PEPPER to taste
- ❒ Large Saute Pan
- ❒ Spoon

Method of Preparation

In a large saute pan, over medium heat, saute 1/8 teas minced GARLIC in 1/2 Tbls BUTTER.

Add 1 1/4 qts WHIPPING CREAM and 6 oz TOMATO SAUCE.

Bring to a boil. Then reduce the heat.

Now add:

- 1/2 cup Grated ROMANO CHEESE
- 1/8 cup Fresh chopped BASIL LEAVES.
- 1 oz CHICKEN STOCK
- SALT and BLACK PEPPER to taste

Let simmer until desired thickness is achieved and serve.

THE NEPHEW'S NEW ENGLAND CLAM CHOWDER

Servings - 8

A Superb winter dish.

INGREDIENTS AND UTENSILS

- ❒ 1 1/2 RUSSET POTATOES, peeled and cut into 1/4 inch pieces
- ❒ 3 oz diced SLAB BACON
- ❒ 1/4 Jumbo Yellow ONION, coarsely chopped
- ❒ 1 1/2 qts Heavy WHIPPING CREAM
- ❒ 14 oz canned or bottled CLAM JUICE
- ❒ 3/4 lb minced CLAMS

INGREDIENTS FOR ROUX

- ❒ 4 oz BUTTER
- ❒ 3 oz FLOUR
- ❒ Knife and Cutting Board
- ❒ Stock Pot
- ❒ Measuring utensils

METHOD OF PREPARATION

In the stock pot, saute 3 oz SLAB BACON for 3 - 4 minutes. Add 1/4 Jumbo Yellow ONION and saute for additional 4 minutes.

Add:

- 1 1/2 qts WHIPPING CREAM
- 1 1/2 Russet POTATOES, coarse chopped
- 14 oz canned CLAM JUICE
- 12 oz minced CLAMS

Now, make a ROUX, by heating 4 oz BUTTER, and adding 3 oz FLOUR gradually, stirring for at least 3 minutes.

Add ROUX to the Chowder, and cook over very low heat for 1 1/2 hours. Stir often to make sure that soup does not scorch.

THE NEPHEW'S ASPARAGUS SOUP

Servings - 4

Ingredients and Utensils

- ❒ 1/2 lb Fresh ASPARAGUS
- ❒ 3/4 qt Heavy WHIPPING CREAM
- ❒ 1/8 Tbls Minced Peeled GARLIC
- ❒ 1/2 Tbls CHICKEN STOCK
- ❒ Pinch of SALT and BLACK PEPPER
- ❒ Large Pot
- ❒ Cutting board and spoon
- ❒ Sharp Knife
- ❒ Blender
- ❒ Measuring cups and spoons

Method of Preparation

In a large pot, heat 3/4 qt of Heavy WHIPPING CREAM and 1/2 Tbls CHICKEN STOCK.

Cut off bottom of the ASPARAGUS STALKS *(unusable part)* Take 2 oz of the ASPARAGUS and cut into 2 inch pieces and set aside.

Blanch the balance of the Asparagus in boiling water for about 5 minutes.

Take the 1/8 Tbls Minced GARLIC and the blanched Asparagus and beat in a blender. Stir into a simmering liquid, add asparagus pieces, SALT and PEPPER to taste.

Simmer and serve.

PART EIGHT: DESSERTS

The magic touch of Sweets

The Nephew and the Old Uncle sat in the office of the D'AMICO Italian Market Café.

"Old Uncle, tell me about the desserts you plan for our new book."

"I got it all figured out, dear Nephew. First, though, let's have some coffee. Brina, darling, can you handle that tough assignment?"

Brina, the Nephew's beautiful daughter, who finished college with a degree in the restaurant catering business, quickly brought the coffee to the Old Uncle, his wife of 58 years, Esther Mae, and to her Dad. Esther Mae is the Nephew's Aunt, being the sister of his Dad.

"Nephew, that section of desserts in the first book was something else. I want to bring back three of those. The Italian Fig Cookie, a staple of Italian people, the Biscotti, a cookie made with many recipes, and the unbelievable Amaretto Cream Cake. As for you, my dear Nephew, The Cannoli is a standout, so I know you will bring that back. Now, what else, young fellow?"

The Nephew broke into a laugh.

"Old man, you got it all figured out. I guess being eighty years old might help. By gosh, you're right, but I need to add my new dessert sensation, the Tiramisu. I think those are outstanding."

"Nephew, you're absolutely right, for once."

This brought a laugh from everyone.

THE NEPHEW'S TIRAMISU

Servings - 8

Ingredients and Utensils

- ❒ 1 lb Imported MASCARPONE CHEESE
- ❒ 1 pt WHIPPING CREAM
- ❒ 11 EGG YOLKS from large eggs
- ❒ 1/2 cup SUGAR
- ❒ 3 Tbls POWDERED SUGAR
- ❒ 6 oz MARSALA WINE
- ❒ 7 oz LADY FINGERS
- ❒ 1 1/2 cups ESPRESSO brewed COFFEE
- ❒ 1 1/2 oz KAHLUA LIQUEUR
- ❒ Grated Chocolate Chips
- ❒ Sliced STRAWBERRIES for garnish
- ❒ 9 x 12 x 2 inch Pan for 8 servings.
- ❒ Small Pasta type bowl

Method of Preparation

In a 9 x 12 x 2 inch pan, line up 7 oz of LADY FINGERS. Pour 1 1/2 cups of ESPRESSO COFFEE, and let it soak into the Lady Fingers.

Over boiling water, mix :

- 11 EGG YOLKS
- 1/2 cup Granulated SUGAR
- 6 oz MARSALA WINE

whipping continuously until frothy.

Spread this mixture over the soaked lady fingers. Now make a cream filling by combining 1 pt WHIPPING CREAM, 1 lb Imported MASCARPONE CHEESE, 1 1/2 oz KAHLUA LIQUEUR, and 3 Tbls POWDERED SUGAR. Mix until smooth. Spread filling to make top layer of the Tiramisu. Now chill.

Before serving, grate CHOCOLATE CHIPS and slice STRAWBERRIES over the dessert.

THE NEPHEW'S CANNOLI

Servings - 12

This crown jewel of Italian Desserts freezes well, so we believe it is worth the little extra trouble to make some for the freezer. The Shells - The completed Cannoli shells can be found in specialty food stores and in first class bakeries. They are easily made, if you so desire to do, but you must acquire the small cannoli tubes. A restaurant supplier can furnish you the tubes at minimum cost. If you prefer, you could buy just six and make half a recipe.

INGREDIENTS AND UTENSILS

To Make the Shells:

- ❒ 1 lb All Purpose FLOUR
- ❒ 1 Large EGG
- ❒ 1/4 cup granulated SUGAR
- ❒ 1 1/2 teas Ground CINNAMON
- ❒ 1 cup LAMBRUSCO WINE
- ❒ 1 1/4 oz BUTTER
- ❒ Deep Fryer
- ❒ Oil for frying
- ❒ Mixing bowl, Rolling pin, Cannoli tubes

To make the Cannoli Stuffing:

- 1 1/2 lbs RICOTTA CHEESE (Part Skim)
- 1/2 cup CHOPPED PISTACHIO NUTS
- 1/4 cup CHOCOLATE CHIPS
- 1/2 lb drained CANDIED FRUIT *(chopped well by hand)*
- 1 1/2 teas VANILLA
- 1/2 teas ALMOND EXTRACT
- 5 oz POWDERED SUGAR

Chopping board and sharp knife,
Mixing bowl and spoon

To build the Cannoli:
In addition to the shells and the stuffing, you will need a few sliced or slivered ALMONDS and POWDERED SUGAR for dipping and sprinkling

THE NEPHEW'S CANNOLI

Continued

Method of Preparation

First, the shells: Measure and add all the below ingredients in a large bowl.

- 1 lb All Purpose FLOUR
- 1 Large EGG
- 1/4 teas Granulated SUGAR
- 1 1/2 teas ground CINNAMON
- 1 cup LAMBRUSCO WINE
- 1 1/4 oz BUTTER

Mix well to form dough. Turn out on a board and knead well. Roll out until thin, then cut into 3 1/2 inch squares. Lay out squares until they face you as diamonds. Place the cannoli tube lengthwise on the square *(north and south)* Bring up opposite points *(east and west)* across the tube and join together using some egg wash. Using Oil, fry in Deep Fryer about 360 degrees or in skillet on medium heat. Until golden brown.

Second, the Stuffing: Combine all the ingredients below and mix well.

- 1 1/2 lbs RICOTTA CHEESE *(part skim)*
- 1/2 cup PISTACHIO NUTS, chopped
- 1/4 cup CHOCOLATE CHIPS
- 1/2 cup chopped CANDIED FRUIT *(chopped well by hand)*
- 1 1/2 teas VANILLA
- 1/2 teas ALMOND EXTRACT
- 5 oz POWDERED SUGAR

Refrigerate until needed.

THE NEPHEW'S CANNOLI

Continued

Third, Building the Cannoli: Using a spoon, fill each shell with about a half cup of the stuffing.

When completed, dip each end of the Cannoli into the toasted or slivered almonds. Lastly, sprinkle well with Powdered Sugar. Refrigerate for present use or freeze for later.

Cannoli

Tiramisu

THE OLD UNCLE'S BISCOTTI

Servings - Makes about 70 cookies at the recommended size below. My wife and I usually make a half recipe.

Known as the Italian Vanilla Wafer, the Biscotti recipe below is considered superior to any vanilla wafer.

Note - A smooth as silk cookie. Keeps well in a can or wrapped in plastic.

Ingredients and Utensils

- ❒ 1 1/4 cups Granulated SUGAR
- ❒ 1 cup CANOLA OIL *(or shortening)*
- ❒ 2 Large EGGS, slightly beaten
- ❒ 2 teas VANILLA
- ❒ 1/2 cup MILK *(skim works fine)*
- ❒ 5 cups FLOUR
- ❒ 3 1/2 teas BAKING POWDER
- ❒ VEGETABLE SPRAY
- ❒ Large bowl for mixing
- ❒ Knife
- ❒ Rolling pin and board
- ❒ Cookie Sheets

Method of Preparation

In a large bowl, blend together:

- 1 1/4 cups Granulated SUGAR
- 1 cup CANOLA OIL

Adding:

- 2 beaten EGGS
- 2 teas VANILLA
- 1/2 cup MILK

When finished, sift and add to the above:

- 5 cups FLOUR
- 3 1/2 teas BAKING POWDER

This should make a medium dough, but if it feels too soft, add a little flour

When dough feels right, either roll out with a rolling pin, or smooth down with your hands.

THE OLD UNCLE'S BISCOTTI

Continued

Cut into strips about 1 inch wide and 1/4 inch thick.

Slice into cookies, about 2 1/2 inches long. Cut 2 slits and twist each end of each cookie.

Spray cookie sheet or sheets with VEGETABLE SPRAY. Space cookies out as preferred.

Bake at 350 degrees for ten minutes. Check the bottoms, if getting dark, and still too light on top, take them out anyway.

Some people like these cookies crisp. If they are not crisp enough for your preference, next time make them thinner.

The Old Uncle's Greatgrandaughters, Emily & Anilise.

THE OLD UNCLE'S ITALIAN CREAM CAKE

Servings 12

Ingredients and Utensils

- ❒ 2 prepared 9" YELLOW CAKE LAYERS
- ❒ 1/2 cup CORNSTARCH
- ❒ 1 cup SUGAR
- ❒ 2 1/4 cups MILK
- ❒ 3 beaten EGGS
- ❒ 1 teas VANILLA
- ❒ 1 teas RUM EXTRACT
- ❒ 1 cup APRICOT BRANDY *(Divided into 3/4 and 1/4 cups)*
- ❒ 12 oz jar APRICOT PRESERVES
- ❒ 2 cups HEAVY CREAM
- ❒ Sharp Knife
- ❒ Medium Sauce Pan or Casserole dish
- ❒ Cake Plate
- ❒ Mixing Bowl
- ❒ Bow Knife

Method of Preparation

In a sauce pan, add:

- 1/2 cup CORNSTARCH
- 1 cup SUGAR

On low heat, Stir and add:

- 2 1/4 cups MILK
- 3 beaten EGGS

Continue stirring until pudding bubbles.

Cool, then add :

- 1 teas VANILLA
- 1 teas RUM EXTRACT

Refrigerate.

THE OLD UNCLE'S ITALIAN CREAM CAKE

Continued

Divide each YELLOW CAKE Layer in half. Sprinkle all parts of the cake layers with the 3/4 cup of Apricot Brandy, Spread the 12 oz jar of APRICOT PRESERVES over the bottom 3 layers. Spread the refrigerated custard mixture over the Apricot Preserves.

Now, combine by stacking the layers.

In a large bowl, beat 2 cups HEAVY CREAM until stiff, gradually adding the 1/4 cup of APRICOT BRANDY.

Spread over the entire cake and refrigerate.

Guaranteed satisfaction.

The Old Uncles, father, in full Cook's regalia.

The Old Uncle (left) and his father, at the family bakery.

THE OLD UNCLE'S ITALIAN FIG COOKIES

Servings - This recipe makes 10 dozen. (2- 2 1/2 inches) They freeze remarkable well uncooked. Enjoy fresh delicious Fig morsel anytime you so desire. Freeze on a Flat Pan, then put the cookies in a plastic bag once frozen solid. Cook without thawing whenever.

Note - A famous Italian cookie for many generations. Usually made for St. Joseph's Altar Tables -(March 19th) and for Christmas.

Ingredients and Utensils

- ❒ 3 - 8 oz Pkgs DRIED FIGS
- ❒ 1 - LARGE ORANGE
- ❒ 2 - teas CINNAMON
- ❒ 1 1/2 cups HONEY
- ❒ 6 cups FLOUR
- ❒ 2 cups VEGETABLE SHORTENING
- ❒ 1/2 cup SUGAR
- ❒ 2 or 2 1/2 cups WATER
- ❒ VEGETABLE SPRAY
- ❒ 2 oz MILK *(for brushing)*
- ❒ Electric or hand grinder
- ❒ Cutting board and knife
- ❒ Large bowl or pan to mix dough in
- ❒ Rolling pin and bread board
- ❒ Cookie sheet for baking and freezing

Method of Preparation

Although the cookies can easily be made in one day, we prefer to make the filling one day, refrigerate it, and finish them the next day.

Cut off the stems of the three 8oz bags of DRIED FIGS.

Cut up the Large ORANGE. Depending on the type of orange used, cut up the outside part of the rind in small pieces. The meat of the orange should also be used but not necessarily in as small pieces as the outside of the rind.

Using the grinder, combine the figs, orange pieces, and the small rind pieces together and grind once.

THE OLD UNCLE'S ITALIAN FIG COOKIES

To the mixture add 2 teaspoons CINNAMON, and 1/2 cup HONEY. Mix and grind again. Now add the remaining 1 cup of HONEY and mix well.

At this point, refrigerate the mixture. If you want to call it a day, fine. If not, refrigerate it long enough to mix the dough.

The Old Uncle and his champion Labrador retriever, Toto.

In a large bowl or pan, add:

- 6 cups FLOUR
- 2 cups VEGETABLE SHORTENING
- 1/2 cup SUGAR

Mix, gradually adding 2 to 2 1/2 cups WATER. (Mixing by hand, add one cup and then In small amounts, gradually add the water until the dough becomes smooth. Cover dough with a damp cloth, and remove fig mixture from the refrigerator.

Roll out the mixture in 1/2 inch strips. *(It will be sticky!)* Cut off a good handful of dough. Roll out to a thin rectangle. Place rolled mixture in the center of the strips. *(Again it will be sticky)* You can do it!

Carefully roll the dough partially over the filling from one side. Then let it overlap from the other side, leaving the seam on the bottom.

Spray the sheet pans with Vegetable Spray. Cut rolled dough and filling into 2 1/2" pieces. Cut two small slits on each cookie, and flatten them a little.

Place on baking sheets, usually 11 x 17, and bake at 350 degrees for about 15 minutes. Be sure you WATCH THEM CAREFULLY! Ovens vary in heat temperatures. GOOD LUCK!

The Nephew and all his first cousins in the driveway on Terry Street, Houston.. From left to right: Nash D'Amico Jr., Frankie Petronella, Frank D'Amico, David Consoli and Vincent Consoli.

The Nephew's Uncle Sam (Dad's twin brother) with Great-Grandmother Margarite LaMatta, in front of the families home Polk Street.

The Nephew's Mom and Dad, in the early days.

SECTION TWO
FAMILY

FAMILY

Family loyalty is a strong point of the Italian people. While this is true of many other nationalities, it is certainly still something to be very proud of. The Nephew and the Old Uncle present the following information on their families, hoping you would be interested in reading this page about it. We offer some recipes from the two families, so maybe you would get a kick out of making an old recipe. Over the years, Italian people remain joyful and happy that the Vatican has remained in Italy for so many years. Today, Italy is one of the leaders in fashion designs, as all types of clothing and shoes are sold worldwide. However, it is the reputation of their foods that many of us look to. The foods and wines of this fabulous land stand out. Most Italian Americans, along with all other nationalities, plan vacations in Italy and Sicily. Nothing can be finer, believe me.

Frank, Paula, Nash, Jr. & Sammy - The D'Amico siblings at Piazza Novona in Rome.

The D'Amico family on a scenic Siclian hillside.

FAMILY BACKGROUND OF THE NEPHEW

The Nephew in this book is Nash D'Amico, Jr. He is the son of Nash D'Amico, Sr. (deceased) and Rosalie Pizzitola D'Amico. Both are true Houstonians, being born and raised in Houston. Nash, Sr. was an accountant, while Rosalie was a housewife. Their family consists of three sons and one daughter. Nash, Jr.'s grandparents were Frank D'Amico and Jennie Ingrando D'Amico, and Charles Pizzitola and Pauline Calma Pizzitola, all being born and raised in Houston. Nash, Jr. was quick to point out that he is the only member of his family that has ever been in the food business. Frank D'Amico was a printer and Jennie, a housewife. Charles Pizzitola was a barber, and Pauline, a housewife.

Young Nash, Jr. takes a lesson from Coach Dad. Brother Frank watches from the foreground.

FAMILY BACKGROUND OF THE OLD UNCLE.

The Old Uncle in this book is Paul Joe Provenzano. Paul's wife of 58 years, is Esther Mae D'Amico Provenzano, sister of Nash Jr.'s father. They raised one son. Paul and Esther were both born in Houston and lived their entire life in South Texas. Paul was in the bakery business with his Dad, later went into the wholesale liquor business, was a taxidermist, and is an author. Esther has been a housewife, but also was a cake decorator, and a taxidermist. He is the son of Joe M. Provenzano (deceased) and Jennie Mortellra Provenzano (deceased). Both were born and raised in the Houston area. Joe was a baker, and owned the Louisiana Bakery in Houston for many years. Jennie was a housewife, and they raised three sons. Paul's grandparents were Pasquale Provenzano and Agnes Ligotino Provenzano, and Vince Mortellra and Fannie Pelatari Mortellra Santamaria. All four are deceased. Pasquale and Agnes were born in Sicily. Vince was born in Italy, while Fannie was born in New Orleans. Mortellra was killed at an early age (33 years) in an accident, being thrown from a wild horse. Fannie had two daughters by Mortellra, and two sons and one daughter by Joseph Santamaria. Pasquale operated a grocery store, and Agnes was a housewife. They raised seven children, three being born in Sicily, and four in the U.S. Both of Fannie Mortellra Santamaria's husbands were farmers.

Frank D'Amico served as a cook in WWI.

RECIPES FROM THE FAMILIES

All four of The Nephew's Grandparents, D'Amico & Pizzitola.

PASTA AND PEAS

by Pauline Pizzitola (The Nephews Grandmother)

Boil 2 1/2 qts Water with a little Salt and Olive Oil added.

When boiling, add 8 oz Vermicelli Pasta, breaking the nested pasta into the boiling water. Cook a few minutes, until aldente.

When cooked, pour a little of the water off the top, leaving about 2 qts of water in with the Vermicelli.

Add

- 15 oz can Peas
- 1/3 cup of Olive Oil,
- 2 teas of Black Pepper.

Cook about 5 or 10 minutes longer until very hot, and serve with Grated Romano Cheese sprinkled over it.

The Nephew's mother and father (far right foreground), along with friends and cousins, enjoy a popular night club on South Main in Houston.

BRACIOLA

By Jennie D'Amico (The Nephew's Grandmother)

On a large wooden Board, place:

- One 1 1/2 lbs Round steak *(1/2 inch thick)*, previously tenderized.

Lay it out flat, and cover with the following ingredients:

- 1 cup Italian Seasoned Bread Crumbs
- 3 Tbls Cilantra chopped
- 3 pieces Bacon, chopped in 1/2" pieces
- 3 Tbls Grated Romano Cheese
- 1 Hard Boiled Egg, chopped well
- 5 Hard Boiled Eggs, lined up together, in the center of the steak.
- Sprinkle with Salt and Pepper.

Carefully roll it up keeping the Eggs in a straight line.

Now, tie it in three places to keep it together.

Brown in a skillet with Olive Oil, turning it to brown it all around.

Now, leaving it in the same skillet, cover it well with Italian Red Sauce, either made from recipes in this book or store bought. Bake in the oven at 325 degrees, *(1 1/2 - 2 hrs)* Cook until very tender .Sprinkle with Grated Romano Cheese. Slice and Serve.

The Sicilian slang word for this recipe is pronounced BRU-SHA-LUNA.

SALMON PATTIES

By Rosalie D'Amico (The Nephews Mother)

Mix together:

- 1 - 15 oz can Salmon
- 10 Crackers, crushed
- 1/4 cup Finely chopped Onions
- 1 beaten Egg
- Salt and Pepper

After mixing well, roll in Cracker Meal. Spray a skillet with Vegetable Spray, add 2 Tbls Olive Oil and saute.

HOME MADE BREAD

by Jennie Provenzano (The Old Uncle's Mother)
Considered by her Family and Friends to have been an outstanding cook.

Recipe makes 4 loaves

INGREDIENTS

- ❒ 3 cups warm water
- ❒ 2 pkg Dry Yeast
- ❒ 2 teas Cornmeal
- ❒ 3 Eggs
- ❒ 3/4 cup plus 2 Tbls Sugar
- ❒ 1/2 cup plus 2 Tbls Oil
- ❒ 3/4 teas Salt
- ❒ 9 - 10 cups Flour

In a large bowl, combine 3 cups of warm water and two envelopes of dry Yeast. Let it stand for a few minutes.
Add:

- 2 teas Cornmeal
- 3 Eggs
- 3/4 Cup plus 2 Tbls Sugar

Mix well.

HOME MADE BREAD

by Jennie Provenzano (The Old Uncle's Mother)

Add:

- 1/2 cup plus 2 Tbls Oil
- 3/4 teas Salt

Mix and add 3 cups Flour.

Mix this amount of flour well before adding the balance *(6 or 7 cups).* Empty out on a well floured board, and knead for 8 to 10 minutes. Work until very smooth. Then punch down, roll into a large ball, cover with cloth, and let it rise for 30 to 45 minutes until it seems to be about twice the size. Punch it down, fold it over, and let rest 10 minutes.

Divide into four pieces. Knead and shape each one into a ball. Cover again and let it rest for 20 minutes. Now shape into the desired loaf shape wanted. If you want round bread, simply roll it into a ball, and place on a greased flat pan. If you prefer loaf bread, grease the loaf pans, mold the dough into the shape of the pans and you are in business.

Bake loaf bread at 375 degrees for 30 minutes. Round Bread takes 5 - 10 minutes longer. I use melted butter on top for a soft crust. Remember, practice makes perfect, but it won't take long here.

Frank and Jennie D'Amico in the old days.

ESTHER MAE'S CHEESECAKE

By Esther Mae Provenzano (The Old Uncle's Wife)

INGREDIENTS

- ❒ 1 - 10 inch Graham Cracker Crust *(Store bought is fine)*
- ❒ 2 - 8 oz Pkg. Cream Cheese, softened
- ❒ 1 - 15 oz Can Evaporated Condensed Milk
- ❒ 1 - teas Vanilla
- ❒ 1 - Tbls Sugar
- ❒ 3 - Eggs, slightly beaten

TOPPING:

- ❒ 1/4 cup Sour Cream
- ❒ 1/4 cup Plain Yogurt
- ❒ 3 1/2 Tbls Sugar
- ❒ 1 Tbls Lemon Juice
- ❒ 1/2 cup drained Crushed Pineapple

METHOD :

In a Mixing bowl, place:

- Cream Cheese
- Evaporated Condensed Milk
- Vanilla
- Sugar
- Eggs

Blend well in the mixer, and pour into the Graham Cracker Crust.

Cook in a 300 degree oven for 25 minutes. Meanwhile, in a medium bowl, combine:

- Sour cream
- Plain yogurt
- Sugar
- Lemon juice
- Pineapple

ESTHER MAE'S CHEESECAKE

By Esther Mae Provenzano (The Old Uncle's Wife)

Mix and set aside.

Remove cheese cake from the oven very carefully. Add the topping mix slowly and carefully. Replace in the oven for 10 minutes.

When ready, again remove from the oven very carefully. You should slide it onto a flat board or pan and balance it very carefully.

When cool, refrigerate for at least 4 hours or overnight before serving.

The Old Uncle's lovely wife, Esther Mae, in drum majorette uniform.

FOOLISHNESS

Do you realize what Foolishness is? Maybe you do, but maybe we don't. Obviously, in the food business, we think there are lots of ways to look at it. Look at it this way. If you are a dyed in the wool Italian Cook, it's highly possible that some other type foods could be looked at as Foolishness. Not that this Italian Cook would not eat this type food, but he still could address it as foolishness food.

Maybe you think the above paragraph is foolishness. Hey, you're probably right So, now what? Hell, I don't know. And I'll bet you don't either.

We're not getting anywhere, and if I don't make more sense, you are going to pass this up at any second. True? I thought so.

So, here is what we're going to do. Could you use a Cajun Recipe that glorifies a SEAFOOD GUMBO? Ah-ha! You like that, so go ahead and admit it. After that we'll add on a Tex Mex Recipe known as CHILI. If you got some real toughness in your throat, you will probably love it, and if not, you won't make the grade.

Going back to Louisiana cooking, if you don't complain too much, we are coming with a true OYSTER LOAF. Yeah, that's what I said. So, if you don't like oysters, use fried fish, shrimp, soft shell crabs or whatever. Just don't complain.

How about some Oriental Food. So maybe you like it and maybe you don't. If not pass it up, but we're going to give you a recipe for EGG ROLLS. Yeh, Eggrolls. Nobody is forcing you to make egg rolls, but something tells me you will.

On the other side from where the Tex Mex Chili dish came from, is Old Mexico. The land of the Senoritas and highly seasoned foods. You want the Senoritas? Now, you're on your own. But we'll help you with some hot food. ENCHILADAS. So you won't complain too much, we'll make it an easy one with a fantastic taste.

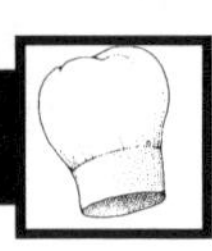

Let's see now. You have recipes from the Cajun Country, Tex Mex Area, Louisiana, The Orient, and Mexico. If you're upset with me, I have some special prizes for you. If you are not upset with me, you get the prizes anyway.

You're suspicious, probably because of this being the foolishness section. While you could be right, you're not.

We are awarding you THE STATE OF TEXAS BREAKFAST SPECIALS. Count them — One - BUTTERMILK BISCUITS, two — PANCAKES, and three — SOUR DOUGH WAFFLES. No Foolishness here. Go ahead and admit it. One more thing, we are going to slip in a recipe or two when we think you might need it after a red hot one. You know, sort of a extra special one to help your reputation.

After that first page of Foolishness, remember that this is all in fun. We hope you enjoy it.

The Nephew's 3rd Grade class picture, at St. Anne's Catholic School in Houston.

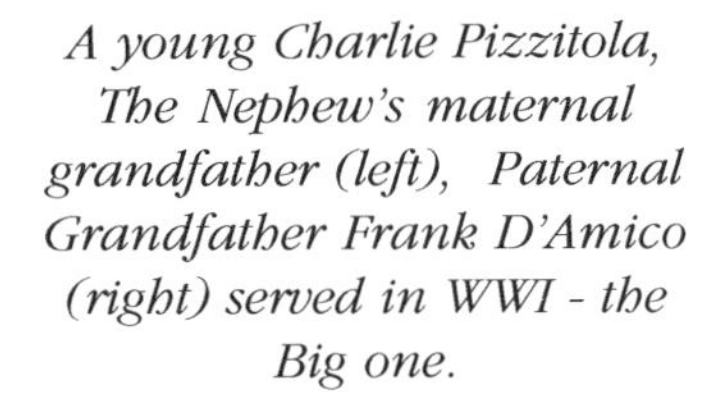

A young Charlie Pizzitola, The Nephew's maternal grandfather (left), Paternal Grandfather Frank D'Amico (right) served in WWI - the Big one.

THE OLD UNCLE'S SEAFOOD GUMBO

Spray a large pot with Vegetable Spray, add:

- 4 Qts Water
- 2 Pkg Dry Gumbo Mix, available in most food stores.
- 6 - 8 Tbls Liquid Roux, available in large chain grocery and specialty stores.
- 1/4 - 1/2 lb Chicken or Turkey Tasso, cut in small pieces. *(Available in specialty stores and large chain stores. Substitute Andoulle Sausage, at same locations.)*
- 5 Tbls Oil
- 1 teas Kitchen Bouquet

Cook for 1 1/2 hours uncovered on low-medium heat

Stir often, making sure it does not stick.

Meanwhile, finely chop the following items, placing in a bowl together:

- 2 Medium to large Bell Peppers
- 2 Medium Onions
- 2 ribs Celery
- 6 cloves Garlic

Then add:

- 1/2 cup Cilantro
- 1/2 teas Ground Cayenne

Add this to the above Roux Mixture after completion of the time allotted. Cook for 1 Hour on simmer after it comes to a boil. Keep covered for now. Stir frequently to keep from sticking.

THE OLD UNCLE'S SEAFOOD GUMBO

Continued

Now, add:

- 2 Tbls Molasses
- 2 Tbls Regular Brandy

Leave uncovered, and simmer. Stir occasionally. Cook for 30 minutes, uncovered.

Add:

- 2 lbs peeled Shrimp
- 1 lb peeled Crawfish Tails
- 1 lb Crab Meat, preferably Fresh.
- 2 Tbls Regular Brandy

Simmer for 30 minutes uncovered.

Serve over rice, if preferred.

The Old Uncle plays in the snow with his brothers, Foley and Joe.

THE OLD UNCLE'S ORIGINAL CHILI

You're back for more Foolishness. Good, GREAT. It'll be interesting to see if you survive this one. Here we go, but first a suggestion. This one is hot so if you have some doubts but want to try it, cut the hot stuff down to half. Either way, let's go!

Vegetable Spray a large pot.

Add :

- 2 Tbls Cooking Oil
- 4 lbs Ground Pork, Beef or Venison. *(If you prefer, ground half in cubes, up to 1/2 inch in diameter)*
- 1 Tbls Onion Powder
- 1 Tbls Garlic Powder
- 1 Tbls Chili Powder
- 2 teas Instant Chicken Bouillon Powder

Cook for 1 1/2 hours on low heat, covered

Add:

- 16 oz Tomato Sauce
- 16 oz Water
- 16 oz Beef Broth
- 2 teas Instant Chicken Bouillon Powder
- 1 Tbls Onion Powder
- 1 Tbls Garlic Powder
- 2 Tbls Chili Powder
- 1 teas Ground Cayenne Powder

Cook for 1 1/2 hours on low heat, uncovered.

THE OLD UNCLE'S ORIGINAL CHILI

Add:

Continued

- 1 Tbls Mexican Oregano
- 1 Tbls Cumin
- 1/2 cup chopped Parsley
- 1/2 cup chopped Cilantro
- 1 Tbls Chili Powder
- 2 teas Molasses
- 2 Tbls Regular Brandy
- 1 1/2 teas Salt.

(Now is the time to check the seasonings. You might prefer more salt, maybe something else. Do it now.)

Cook for only 30 minutes, uncovered. We serve this with Hot Tamales and Tortillas. The Chili freezes very well.

The Old Uncle's Great-grandfather, Vince Mortadella, in Italian Army uniform.

THE OLD UNCLE'S ORIGINAL BREAD PUDDING

If you survived the Chili Recipe, well, I guess you are entitled to this third recipe that we feel proud of. Bread Pudding. Yeah, and don't say you don't like Bread Pudding. Tell it to someone else.

Mix together, and set aside:

- 14 cups day old EGG BREAD, cut in 1" cubes
- 1 cup store bought yellow cake mix

Mix together the following ingredients, and place in a large pot or pan, previously sprayed with Vegetable Spray:

- 8 Eggs, slightly beaten
- 1 cup Sugar
- 1 cup Dark Brown Sugar
- 2 medium cans Freestone Peaches, chopped
- 1 1/2 cups Pecans, chopped
- 1 1/2 cups Raisins
- *3 Tbls Liquid Roux, mixed in a little warm water until it resembles syrup *(Optional)*
- 2 Tbls Cinnamon
- 2 teas Nutmeg
- 3 Tbls Vanilla

Mix well, add above bread mixture, along with 16 oz *(more or less)* of half and half until it becomes a nice soft mixture.

Finally, add 2 sticks melted Butter and mix well again.

Using your clean hands, place mixture in a 9 x 13 x 2 pan, sprayed with Vegetable Spray. Smooth out evenly. Bake at 350 degrees for 45 minutes, uncovered.

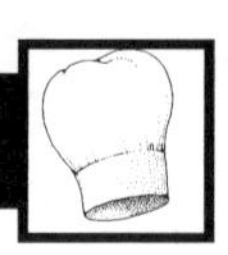

THE OLD UNCLE'S ORIGINAL BREAD PUDDING

Continued

To make the sauce:

Mix together

- 2 sticks melted Butter
- 2 cups Sugar,
- 1 Tbls Vanilla

Blend together, warm, and remove from the fire.

Add:

- 1/2 cup Whiskey or Regular Brandy
- 6 Tbls Whipping Cream or Half & Half

It's ready.

Great-grandmother Ester and Great-grandfather Sam.

THE OLD UNCLE'S CRAB EGG ROLLS

You've probably heard all your life that Eggrolls are hard to make. Absolutely not true. A little time, yes, but actually an easy recipe, with delicious dividends.

There are two items that need to be purchased at an Oriental Food Market.

One a package of 25, Frozen Spring Roll Wrappers.

The second is not frozen. Vermicelli egg noodles or long vermicelli. They come in a single package or in a carton of four. There are about 2 or 3 oz of dried vermicelli in each package.

Soak a package of the Vermicelli Noodles in some cool water for thirty minutes.

Meanwhile, in a saute pan, place

- 1/4 cup Onion, finely chopped
- 1/4 cup Cilantro, chopped
- 1 cup shredded White Cabbage
- 1 Pkg Vermicelli Noodles, soaked and broken into small pieces

Season with Garlic Powder, Salt, and Black Pepper.

Saute for 3 or 4 minutes.

Add 1 lb Fresh Crab Meat, checked closely for broken shell pieces.

Season with Garlic Powder, Salt, and Black Pepper.

Saute for 3 or 4 more minutes and remove from the fire.

Place in a large Bowl.

Add:

- 1 Tbls Sesame Oil
- 1 heaping teas Sesame Seeds
- 2 beaten eggs

Season again with Garlic Powder, Salt, and Black Pepper.

This should make about 25 small to medium egg rolls.

THE OLD UNCLE'S CRAB EGG ROLLS

Continued

Carefully peel the thawed frozen spring roll shells. Since there are 25 to a package, it could come out great. Paint Sesame Oil around the border of each wrapper, and place a heaping tablespoon or a little more of the mixture. Carefully wrap it in the wrapper, pulling it down from the top, then folding over the sides and then finish rolling it up. Not as hard as it sounds. Most packages have directions on them about the folding etc. Now, to the frying. Heat the Oil to 360-375 Degrees. If you don't have a thermometer, guess but be sure it's hot. And be careful, it's easy to get burned. Fry them for 3 or so minutes. You'll be glad you tried it, believe me.

The Old Uncle's father, Joe Provenzano, in WWI uniform

THE NEPHEW'S ENCHILADAS

And now for a trip to Old Mexico. This food may be considered foolishness in an Italian book but we know better about all these classics. Good HOT food with a taste of old Mexico.

In a large saute pan place 4 Tbls Oil, and add:

- 1 1/4 lbs chopped cooked Chicken Breast meat
- 1 lb finely chopped Red Onions
- 1 Fresh Avocado, chopped
- 1 Tbls Ground Coriander
- 1 Fresh Jalapeno, cleaned, seeded, and chopped fine

Saute for 2-3 minutes.

Add:

- 1/4 cup Grated Cheddar Cheese
- 1 - 10 oz can Enchilada Sauce

Simmer for 1-2 minutes. Remove from fire.

Using Flour Tortillas, 9 inches in diameter, spoon the mixture into the center of the tortilla, and carefully roll each one up, placing each one in a glass or ceramic dish touching.

Now, add on top of the tortillas:

- 8 oz sliced Mushrooms
- 1/2 cup Grated Monterrey Jack Cheese
- 1 - 10 oz can Enchilada Sauce

Bake in a 350 degree oven for 15 minutes. Enjoy.

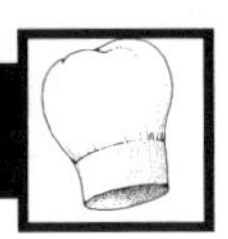

THE OLD UNCLE'S BUTTERMILK BISCUITS

Sift :

- 2 cups of All Purpose FLOUR
- 2 teas BAKING POWDER
- 1/2 teas BAKING SODA
- 1 teas SALT

Mix together.

Add 1/3 cup SHORTENING. Use your hands or some type gadget to incorporate the shortening into the Flour mixture.

The next ingredient is 3/4 cup BUTTERMILK. This is where you make or break the quality of the biscuits.

Pour half of the 3/4 cup of Buttermilk the first time, slightly mix it, then add half the balance, and finally, the rest of it. The less you mix it, the more tender they will be, so mix it very little between the pourings.

Bake in a preheated oven of 425 degrees for ten to twelve minutes.

The Old Uncle beside his first place award from the National Taxidermists.

THE OLD UNCLE'S PANCAKES

In a medium bowl, place:

- 2 cups All Purpose FLOUR
- 2 Tbls BAKING POWDER
- 1 teas BAKING SODA
- 1 teas SALT

In a large bowl, place

- 2 Tbls SUGAR
- 2 EGGS, slightly beaten
- 1/3 cup OIL

Mix, and gradually add:

- 2 cups Canned SKIM MILK

Now add the flour mixture, gradually, but do not over mix.

Cook on regular Pancake Griddle.

The Old Uncle's son, Joe, Joe's wife, Linda and their son, Dan dressed in their new Cowboy Shoot-off outfits.

THE OLD UNCLE'S SOUR DOUGH WAFFLES

Start with:
- 1 Pkg. DRY YEAST
- 1/2 cup very warm WATER

Mix and let set for 10 minutes.

Add:
- 1/2 cup lukewarm WATER
- 1 teas SUGAR
- 1 teas YELLOW CORNMEAL
- 1 teas SALT
- 1 cup FLOUR

Mix together, cover, and let sit overnight in a warm place. I put mine on top of the refrigerator.

The next morning, uncover and mix well, with the wooden spoon. If the bowl is big enough, use it.

Add to the complete sponge,
- 3/4 cup MILK
- 1/2 teas SALT
- 3 Tbls OIL
- 1 beaten EGG
- 1 Tbls BAKING POWDER
- 1/2 teas BAKING SODA

Mix together, cover, and let sit for 20 to 30 minutes.

Cook on Belgian or Regular Waffle Iron.

Sour Dough Waffles ? You may have heard of them but probably not. Anyway, if made right, they are delicious. Remember, Sour Dough is an art, so with the limited space we have, it probably will ring a bell with you.

The biggest problem with sour dough cooking is the sponge. I really don't know why most recipes call for keeping the sponge or starter. The way we are going to do it is easier, and 100 percent successful.

So here we go. First, you must use only glass or ceramic pans or bowls. Your spoon must be wooden. Metal spoons or bowls break down the sour dough, so stay away from them.

RECIPE INDEX

SAUCES

PASTA ENTREES

RECIPE INDEX

MEAT DISHES

SEAFOOD DISHES

VEGETABLES

RECIPE INDEX

ANTIPASTO !

SOUPS

DESSERTS

RECIPE INDEX

The Nephew's FAMILY RECIPES

The Old Uncle's FAMILY RECIPES

FOOLISHNESS RECIPES